Series / Number 07-033

CONFIRMATORY FACTOR ANALYSIS
A Preface to LISREL

J. SCOTT LONG
Washington State University

SAGE PUBLICATIONS
Beverly Hills / London / New Delhi

For information address:

SAGE Publications, Inc.
275 South Beverly Drive
Beverly Hills, California 90212

SAGE Publications India Pvt. Ltd.
C-236 Defence Colony
New Delhi 110 024, India

SAGE Publications Ltd
28 Banner Street
London EC1Y 8QE, England

International Standard Book Number 0-8039-2044-X

Library of Congress Catalog Card Number 83-050185

FIRST PRINTING

When citing a professional paper, please use the proper form. Remember to cite the
correct Sage University Paper series title and include the paper number. One of the
following formats can be adapted (depending on the style manual used):

(1) IVERSEN, GUDMUND R. and NORPOTH, HELMUT (1976) "Analysis of
Variance." Sage University Paper series on Quantitative Application in the Social
Sciences, 07-001. Beverly Hills and London: Sage Pubns.

OR

(2) Iversen, Gudmund R. and Norpoth, Helmut. 1976. *Analysis of Variance.* Sage
University Paper series on Quantitative Applications in the Social Sciences, series no.
07-001. Beverly Hills and London: Sage Pubns.

CONTENTS

Notation

Boldface letters are used to indicate matrices and vectors. For example, B indicates that B is a matrix. Dimensions of matrices and vectors are indicated by "$(r \times c)$" for a matrix with r rows and c columns. Subscripts to lower-case letters indicate elements of a matrix. For example, the $(i,j)^{th}$ element of B is indicated as b_{ij}; the ith element of the vector x is indicated as x_i. The symbol "'" indicates the transpose of a matrix; thus B' is the transpose of B. The symbol "-1" as a superscript of a matrix indicates the inverse of the matrix B; B^{-1} is the inverse of B. "COV" is the covariance operator. If the arguments of the operator are two variables, say x_i and x_j, then $COV(x_i,x_j)$ indicates the covariance between x_i and x_j. If the argument of the covariance operator is a vector, say x of dimension $(n \times 1)$, then $COV(x)$ is the $(n \times n)$ covariance matrix whose $(i,j)^{th}$ element (for $i \neq j$) is the covariance between x_i and x_j, and whose $(i,i)^{th}$ element is the variance of x_i. Similarly, "COR" is used as the correlation operator. $COR(x_i,x_j)$ indicates the correlation between x_i and x_j. $COR(x)$ is the $(n \times n)$ correlation matrix whose $(i,j)^{th}$ element (for $i \neq j$) is the correlation between x_i and x_j, and whose $(i,i)^{th}$ element is one. "E" is the expectation operator. If x_i is a random variable, $E(x_i)$ is the expected value of x_i. If x is a vector, then $E(x)$ is a vector whose i^{th} element is the expected value of the random variable x_i.

Figures, equations, and tables are numbered sequentially within chapters. Thus Table 2.3 is the third table in Chapter 2. The same examples are developed throughout the text and are referred to by the same example number. Thus, if Example 2 is discussed in Chapter 4, the reader should realize that it is a continuation of Example 2 from earlier chapters.

The literature on the confirmatory factor model uses Greek letters. People who have not encountered these "squiggles" before may experience unnecessary anxiety and confusion. For those who have not mastered the Greek alphabet, it is worthwhile to spend some time learning the following Greek letters.

NAMES OF GREEK LETTERS

Upper Case	Lower Case	Name
A	α	alpha
B	β	beta
Γ	γ	gamma
Δ	δ	delta
E	ϵ	epsilon
Z	ζ	zeta
H	η	eta
Θ	θ	theta
I	ι	iota
K	κ	kappa
Λ	λ	lambda
M	μ	mu
N	ν	nu
Ξ	ξ	xi
O	o	omicron
Π	π	pi
P	ρ	rho
Σ	σ	sigma
T	τ	tau
Υ	υ	upsilon
Φ	ϕ	phi
X	χ	chi
Ψ	ψ	psi
Ω	ω	omega

Preface

This monograph presents a statistical method known as confirmatory factor analysis. Two groups of people should find this method to be of interest: first, those who are currently using the more traditional technique of exploratory factor analysis may find that their research problems are more appropriately analyzed with confirmatory factor analysis. Second, those who are interested in the analysis of covariance structures, more commonly known as the LISREL model, will find study of the confirmatory factor model to be a useful first step in understanding the more complex LISREL model. It is for this reason that the monograph has been subtitled *A Preface to LISREL*. Members of the first group are likely to find themselves evolving into members of the second group, since the advantages of the confirmatory factor model over the exploratory factor model are more than equaled by the advantages of the covariance structure model over the confirmatory factor model.

Upon mastery of the materials in this monograph, the reader will be ready to study the more complex covariance structure model. To this end, a second monograph in the Sage series on Quantitative Applications in the Social Sciences is available. This monograph, entitled *Covariance Structure Models: An Introduction to LISREL,* was written in conjunction with the current monograph. The reader of *Confirmatory Factor Analysis* can read *Covariance Structure Models* with no loss of continuity.

Matrix algebra is a necessary prerequisite for studying the confirmatory factor model. While the proofs presented are simple, the reader must feel comfortable with matrix multiplication, inversion, and transposition, and with the distributive property of matrices. Notes at the end of the monograph provide brief reviews for each matrix operation or property when it is used for the first time in the text. Readers who need a more thorough review are encouraged to consult an introductory text in matrix algebra such as Namboodiri (forthcoming) or Chapter 1 of Hohn (1973). The basic statistical concepts presented in texts such as Hays (1981) or Blalock (1979) are also assumed.

A full understanding of the confirmatory factor model requires the application of the model to actual data. Readers are encouraged to replicate the analyses presented in the text. The correlations and standard deviations necessary for such replications are contained in Appendix I. If the results you obtain match those presented in the text, you have a good indication that you understand the confirmatory factor model. To estimate the confirmatory factor model it is generally necessary to use software designed to estimate the covariance structure model (e.g., LISREL, MILS). Appendix II describes how such software can be used to estimate the confirmatory factor model.

A number of people generously gave of their time to comment on various portions of this monograph. I would especially like to thank Paul Allison, Carol Hickman, Karen Pugliesi, Jay Stewart, Blair Wheaton, Ronald Schoenberg, and two anonymous reviewers. The final product is far better for their efforts. Remaining errors and lack of clarity are the result of not heeding the advice of those listed above.

Series Editor's Introduction

I am delighted to write the introduction to this volume. Confirmatory factor analysis is rapidly replacing exploratory factor analysis in social science research, and the LISREL model is now "state of the art" in sociology, psychology, and political science. The interest in these topics, as measured by inquiries from potential authors and from potential readers, far exceeds that expressed in any other topic currently under consideration by the editors and publishers of this series. We are pleased, therefore, to contemplate the pedagogic success of this volume and of its companion volume, *Covariance Structure Models: An Introduction to LISREL*.

Professor Long has written a remarkably lucid and parsimonious introduction to confirmatory factor analysis. Although some familiarity with matrix algebra is required, those whose recollection of matrices is a bit rusty will find enough refresher material presented in this monograph to proceed without delay. Those who are truly novices with matrices will find it necessary to consult an introductory volume such as Namboodiri's *Matrix Algebra* (forthcoming in this series). No other formal background is required beyond the usual exposure to introductory statistical materials.

I personally find that Professor Long's presentational style is so concise and clear, and he makes such judicious use of examples, that even the beginner ought to learn a great deal by reading this monograph. There are many potential obstacles to overcome in learning about the Confirmatory Factor Model (CFM), including the unfamiliar notation and the technical nature of most presentations. Professor Long has gone a great distance toward demystifying the topic. His presentation is technically accurate yet entirely readable.

Confirmatory Factor Analysis presents the basic CFM equations and assumptions, provides a thorough discussion of identification in such models, and compares various methods of statistical estimation, including unweighted least squares, generalized least squares, and maximum likelihood methods. Throughout the manuscript, Professor Long returns to two basic applications of the CFM, the first a general discussion of its application to the multimethod-multitrait model, and the second a discussion of a specific model of psychological disorders. The theoretical advantages of the confirmatory over the exploratory model are emphasized and demonstrated. Professor Long recognizes the increased complexity of the confirmatory model and the special problems it engenders (such as making it more difficult to determine whether a particular model is identified), but he presents sufficient general discussion of the problem, and several examples using procedures to determine identification, to convey to the reader the impression that although the exploratory model solves the identification problem by fiat, it is clearly inferior as a tool for theory testing in the social sciences.

The second volume, *Covariance Structure Models*, builds nicely on this presentation, so the reader can go directly to the more advanced manuscript without difficulty. I suspect that this two-volume set will become a standard reference among social scientists interested in understanding and using factor analysis.

—*John L. Sullivan*
Series Co-Editor

CONFIRMATORY FACTOR ANALYSIS
A Preface to LISREL

J. SCOTT LONG
Washington State University

1. INTRODUCTION

Some variables of theoretical interest cannot be directly observed. This is the fundamental idea underlying the factor analytic model. These unobserved variables are referred to as either *latent* variables or *factors*. While latent variables cannot be directly observed, information about them can be obtained indirectly by noting their effects on *observed* variables. Factor analysis is a statistical procedure for uncovering a (usually) smaller number of latent variables by studying the covariation among a set of observed variables.

Exploratory Versus Confirmatory Factor Analysis

Figure 1.1 illustrates an *exploratory* factor model. In this figure, as in later figures, observed variables are represented by squares and latent variables are represented by circles. A straight arrow pointing from a latent variable to an observed variable indicates the causal effect of the latent variable on the observed variable. Curved arrows between two latent variables indicate that those variables are correlated.

The circles at the top of Figure 1.1 correspond to the latent variables ξ_1, ξ_2, and ξ_3. The curved arrows between these factors indicate that they are correlated with one another. Each of these factors causally affects each of the observed variables, contained in the boxes labeled x_1 to x_7, as indicated by the arrows from the ξ's to the x's. The factors labeled with ξ's are called *common* factors, since their effects are shared in common with more than one of the observed variables. The circles at the bottom of the figure, labeled δ_1 to to δ_7, are called *unique* factors, or errors in variables. Unlike the common factors, their effects are unique to one and only one observed variable. In the exploratory factor model, unique factors are assumed to be uncorrelated with one another and with the common factors, as indicated by the lack of curved arrows between them in Figure 1.1.

The model represented by Figure 1.1 is referred to as an exploratory factor model to reflect the fact that beyond the specifications of the numbers of common factors and observed variables to be analyzed, the researcher does not specify the structure of the relationships among the variables in the model. The researcher must assume that

(1) *all* common factors are correlated (or, in some types of exploratory factor analysis, that *all* common factors are uncorrelated);
(2) *all* observed variables are directly affected by *all* common factors;
(3) unique factors are uncorrelated with one another;
(4) *all* observed variables are affected by a unique factor; and
(5) all ξ's are uncorrelated with all δ's.

These assumptions are made regardless of the substantive appropriateness. Additional and generally arbitrary assumptions must then be imposed in order to estimate the model's parameters. The exploratory factor model's inability to incorporate substantively meaningful constraints, and its necessary imposition of substantively meaningless constraints, has earned it the scornful label of garbage in/garbage out (GIGO) model.

The limitations of the exploratory factor model have been largely overcome by the development of the *confirmatory* factor model (Jöreskog, 1967, 1969; Jöreskog and Lawley, 1968). In the confirmatory factor model, the researcher imposes *substantively motivated* constraints. These constraints determine (1) which pairs of common factors are correlated, (2) which observed variables are affected by which common factors, (3) which observed variables are affected by a unique factor, and (4) which pairs of unique factors are correlated. Statistical tests can be performed to determine if the sample data are consistent with the imposed constraints or, in other words, whether the data *confirm* the substantively generated model. It is in this sense that the model is thought of as confirmatory.

The distinction between exploratory and confirmatory factor models can be seen by comparing the exploratory model in Figure 1.1 to the confirmatory model in Figure 1.2. In the confirmatory model, the

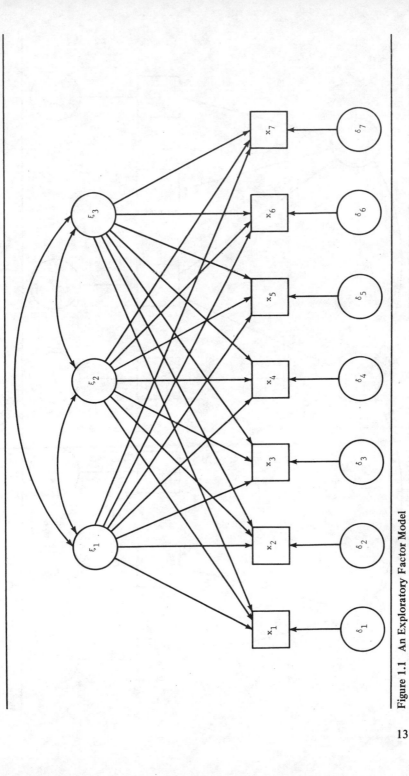

Figure 1.1 An Exploratory Factor Model

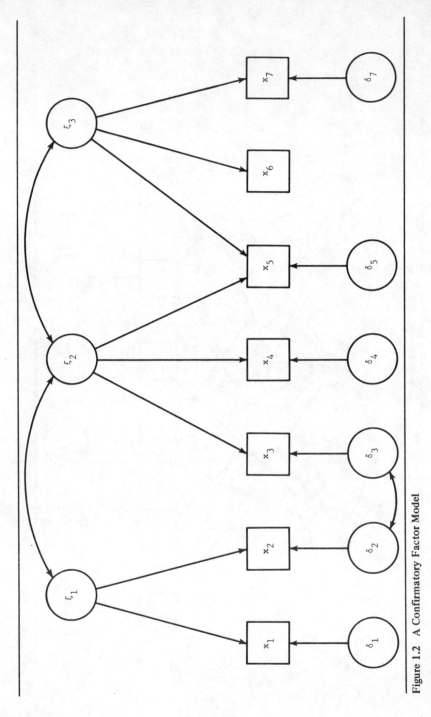

Figure 1.2 A Confirmatory Factor Model

14

common factors ξ_1 and ξ_3 are assumed to be uncorrelated, whereas in the exploratory model all common factors are necessarily assumed to be correlated (or alternatively, they may all be assumed to be uncorrelated). In the confirmatory factor model, the observed variables are affected by only some of the common factors (e.g., x_1 is assumed not to be affected by ξ_2 and ξ_3), whereas all observed variables are affected by all common factors in the exploratory model. In the example of the confirmatory factor model, two of the unique factors are assumed to be correlated (δ_2 and δ_3 are correlated as indicated by the curved arrow connecting them), and one of the observed variables is assumed to have no error factor associated with it (x_6 has no unique factor associated with it), whereas in the exploratory model all unique factors are uncorrelated, and a unique factor is associated with each observed variable.

In practice, the researcher may not have a single, compelling model in mind. Instead, a handful of equally reasonable models may be suggested by substantive theory. Or, the researcher may find that the single model suggested by theory does not fit. In either case, the confirmatory factor model can be used in an exploratory fashion. A specification search (Leamer, 1978) can be conducted in which the selection of a model is based on prior examination of the data. Procedures for the exploratory use of confirmatory factor analysis are presented in Chapter 5.

Structural Relations Among Common Factors

Factor models explain the covariation in a set of observed variables in terms of a (usually) smaller number of common factors. The common factors are often of significant theoretical interest, and accordingly most researchers are interested in the structural relations among these factors. While the confirmatory factor model can provide correlations among common factors, these are generally insufficient for determining the structural parameters of interest. Estimating structural parameters requires the application of a structural equation model to the common factors, in the same way that structural equation models are commonly applied to observed variables. For example, Figures 1.2 and 1.3 contain the same observed and latent variables. Figure 1.3 differs in that it assumes that the common factor ξ_1 causally affects ξ_2 and that ξ_1 and ξ_2 causally affect ξ_3. The incorporation of structural relations among latent variables can be accomplished by what is known as the *covariance structure model* or, more popularly, the LISREL model. This more general model is beyond the scope of the current monograph, but is the subject of the companion volume in this series, *Covariance Structure Models*.

16

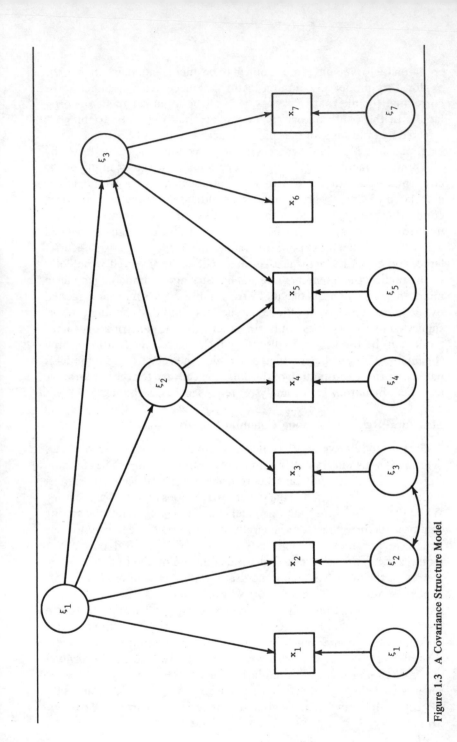

Figure 1.3   A Covariance Structure Model

While the confirmatory factor model is limited by not allowing structural relations among the common factors, it is still an extremely flexible model that can deal with a variety of important applications. These include: (1) measurement models in which latent variables are estimated to eliminate errors in measurement; (2) multiple indicator models in which several indicators of each latent variable are available and a factor model is used to determine the correlations among the common factors (an extension of methods for correcting for attenuation); and (3) multimethod-multitrait models in which each substantive factor is measured with several methods in the hope of eliminating the distorting effects of the methods of measurement. References to specific applications of the confirmatory factor model are given in the concluding chapter.

Organization of the Monograph

The confirmatory factor model is presented in four steps, corresponding to Chapters 2 through 5. Chapter 2 presents the specification of the mathematical model. This involves formal definitions of the various components of the model and a statement of the assumptions. Since the confirmatory factor model allows the researcher to impose constraints specific to the application at hand, this chapter demonstrates how substantive considerations can be translated into constraints on the model. After a model has been specified, it must be determined if the model is identified, the subject of Chapter 3. Identification involves determining if there is a unique solution for the parameters of the model. If a model is not identified, parameters of the model cannot be estimated, and the specification of the model must be reconsidered. Once identification has been established, estimation can proceed. Chapter 4 considers how information from a sample can be used to obtain estimates of population parameters. After a model has been estimated, an assessment of its fit can be made. This involves conducting hypothesis tests as well as making specification searches. These issues are considered in Chapter 5.

2. SPECIFICATION OF THE CONFIRMATORY FACTOR MODEL

Specification of the confirmatory factor model requires making formal and explicit statements about (1) the number of common factors; (2) the number of observed variables; (3) the variances and covariances among the common factors; (4) the relationships among observed variables and latent factors; (5) the relationships among unique factors and observed variables; and (6) the variances and covariances among the unique factors. The great flexibility of the confirmatory factor model comes from its ability to specify each of these components according to the demands of a given application.

An Informal Introduction

Before providing a formal description, the basic components of the confirmatory factor model are illustrated using a portion of a model analyzed by Wheaton (1978) describing the sociogenesis of psychological disorders. This example is used throughout and is referred to as Example 1.

Example 1: an informal specification. This model measures psychological disorders for a sample of 603 adult heads of household from the Hennepin area of rural Illinois at two points in time (1967 and 1971). Since a single, adequate measure of psychological disorders is not available, a measurement model is proposed in which two latent variables are assumed: psychological disorder at time 1, referred to as ξ_1, and psychological disorder at time 2, referred to as ξ_2. These common factors are represented by the circles at the top of Figure 2.1.

Psychological disorder at each point in time is imperfectly measured by two observed variables. ξ_1 is linked to the number of psychological symptoms at time, 1 x_1, and the number of psychophysiological symptoms at time 1, x_2. Similarly, ξ_2 is linked to the corresponding observed variables x_3 and x_4 measured at time 2. In the terminology of factor analysis, we state that x_1 and x_2 load on ξ_1, and x_3 and x_4 load on ξ_2. The observed variables are indicated by the squares in Figure 2.1, and the loadings are indicated by the *solid*, straight arrows connecting the latent variables to the observed variables. Note that the observed variables do

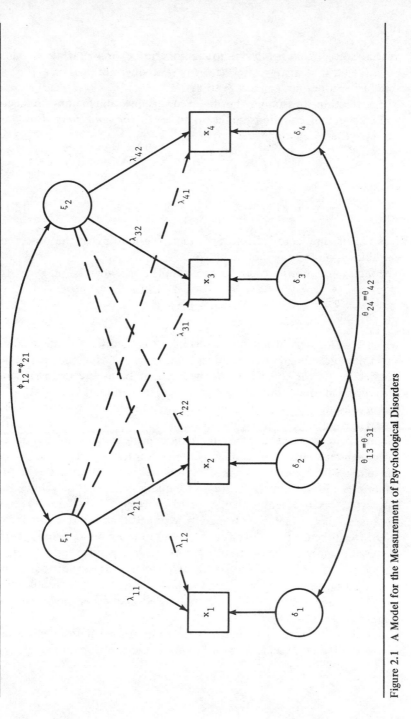

Figure 2.1   A Model for the Measurement of Psychological Disorders

19

not have direct links to all common factors. For example, while x_1 loads on ξ_1 (i.e., a solid arrow connects ξ_1 to x_1), x_1 does not load on ξ_2 (i.e., a solid arrow does not connect ξ_2 to x_1).

The relationships among the observed variables and factors are specified in a set of equations, referred to as *factor equations*. For our example these equations are

$$x_1 = \lambda_{11}\xi_1 + \delta_1 \qquad\qquad x_2 = \lambda_{21}\xi_1 + \delta_2$$

$$x_3 = \lambda_{32}\xi_2 + \delta_3 \qquad\qquad x_4 = \lambda_{42}\xi_2 + \delta_4 \qquad [2.1]$$

δ_i is the unique factor affecting x_i. λ_{ij} is the loading of the observed variables x_i on the common factor ξ_j.

The factor equations are similar to a simple linear regression:

$$Y = \alpha + \beta X + e \qquad [2.2]$$

where Y is an observed dependent variable, X is an observed independent variable, and e is an error term indicating that X does not perfectly predict Y. Factor equations can be thought of as the regression of observed variables (our x's) on unobserved variables (our ξ's). The factor loadings (the λ's in equation 2.1) correspond to slope coefficients (the β in equation 2.2). In equation 2.2, β indicates that a unit change in the independent variable X results in an expected change of β units in the dependent variable Y. Similarly, the factor loadings indicate how a unit change in a common factor affects an observed variable. The factor equations differ from the regression equation in that they have no intercept. Or equivalently, they have an intercept fixed to zero. This is because in factor analysis it is usually assumed that variables are measured from their means, an issue discussed in more detail below. As in regression analysis, the relationship between independent and dependent variables is not exact. This is reflected by the error term e in equation 2.2 and the unique factors δ_i in the factor equations. These unique factors are represented by the circles labeled with δ's at the bottom of Figure 2.1.

If our model were an exploratory factor model, each observed variable would load on each common factor. These additional loadings are represented by *broken arrows* in Figure 2.1. If these loadings were included in our confirmatory model, the resulting factor equations would be

$$x_1 = \lambda_{11}\xi_1 + \lambda_{12}\xi_2 + \delta_1 \qquad x_2 = \lambda_{21}\xi_1 + \lambda_{22}\xi_2 + \delta_2$$

$$x_3 = \lambda_{31}\xi_1 + \lambda_{32}\xi_2 + \delta_3 \qquad x_4 = \lambda_{41}\xi_1 + \lambda_{42}\xi_2 + \delta_4 \qquad [2.3]$$

If these equations were used rather than those in equation 2.1, the loadings would be interpreted as regression coefficients in multiple regression. For example, the loadings in the equation for x_1 would be interpreted as follows: A unit increase in ξ_1 results in an expected increase of λ_{11} units in x_1, holding ξ_2 constant; and, a unit increase in ξ_2 results in an expected increase of λ_{12} units in x_1, holding ξ_1 constant. In our example the decision to use equation 2.1 as opposed to equation 2.3 is based on substantive considerations. If the specification in equation 2.3 were considered preferable, it could have been used. The point distinguishing confirmatory factor analysis from exploratory factor analysis is that equation 2.3 *must* be used in an exploratory analysis, even if the specification in equation 2.1 is substantively preferable.

It is reasonable to expect that the factor representing psychological disorder at time 1 (ξ_1) is correlated with the factor representing psychological disorder at time 2 (ξ_2). A person with a high level of psychological disorder at time 1 would generally be expected to have a high level of psychological disorder at time 2; conversely, a person with a low level of psychological disorder at time 1 would be expected to have a low level of psychological disorder at time 2. The possibility of such a relationship is represented in Figure 2.1 by the curved arrow labeled ϕ_{12} connecting ξ_1 and ξ_2. If ξ_1 and ξ_2 are assumed to have unit variances, ϕ_{12} would correspond to a correlation between ξ_1 and ξ_2; if ξ_1 and ξ_2 are not assumed to have unit variances, ϕ_{12} would correspond to the covariance between ξ_1 and ξ_2.

The unique factors may also be correlated. If δ_1 corresponds to random error in the measurement of psychological symptoms at time 1 (variable x_1), and δ_3 corresponds to random error in the measurement of psychological symptoms at time 2 (variable x_3), these errors in measurement might be correlated over time. That is, large errors in measurement at time 1 might correspond to large errors at time 2, and small errors at time 1 might correspond to small errors at time 2. This possibility is represented by the curved arrow labeled θ_{13} between δ_1 and δ_3. Similarly, covariation between δ_2 and δ_4 is represented by the curved arrow labeled θ_{24}. At this point the confirmatory factor model again distinguishes itself from the exploratory factor model. In the exploratory model all errors in measurement are assumed to be uncorrelated. For this example, this would mean that θ_{13} and θ_{24} would be assumed to equal zero. //[1]

This informal specification of a simple measurement model serves to introduce the basic issues involved in specifying a confirmatory factor model. At this point it is necessary to provide a more formal specification using matrix algebra.

A Formal Specification

Factor analysis attempts to explain the variation and covariation in a set of observed variables in terms of a set of unobserved factors. Each observed variable is conceptualized as a linear function of one or more factors. These factors are of two types: common factors that may directly affect more than one of the observed variables, and unique or residual factors that may directly affect one and only one observed variable. Mathematically the relationship between the observed variables and the factors is expressed as [2]

$$x = \Lambda\xi + \delta \qquad [2.4]$$

where x is a $(q \times 1)$ vector of observed variables; ξ is a $(s \times 1)$ vector of common factors; Λ is a $(q \times s)$ matrix of factor loadings relating the observed x's to the latent ξ's; and δ is a $(q \times 1)$ vector of the residual or unique factors. It is assumed that the number of observed variables in x is greater than the number of common factors in ξ; that is, $q > s$.

Both the observed and latent variables in equation 2.4 are assumed to be measured as deviations from their means. Thus, the expected value of each vector is a vector containing zeros: $E(x) = 0$; $E(\xi) = 0$; and $E(\delta) = 0$.[3] Since this assumption involves only a change in origin, it does not affect the covariances among the variables and, hence, does not limit the flexibility of the model.[4] For example, let U and V be two variables with means μ and v, and let $u = U - \mu$ and $v = V - v$, then $COV(U,V) = COV(u,v)$.[5] Thus, if we are interested in only the covariance between U and V, it does not matter if we use the original variables or the variables measured as deviations from their means. A practical advantage of assuming zero means is that covariances are equivalent to expectations of the products of variables with zero means. Thus, while $E(UV) \neq COV(U,V)$, it holds that (see Note 5)

$$E(uv) = E[(U - \mu)(V - v)] = COV(U,V) = COV(u,v)$$

Assuming zero means for the observed and latent variables in the confirmatory factor model allows us to define the covariance matrix of a vector of variables in terms of expectations of vector products. Let q be a $(n \times 1)$ vector of random variables such that $E(q) = 0$. Let Q be defined as $E(qq')$, where the $(i,j)^{th}$ element of Q is labeled q_{ij}. For example, assume that q contains three variables $(n = 3)$. Then[6]

$$qq' = \begin{bmatrix} q_1 \\ q_2 \\ q_3 \end{bmatrix} [q_1 \ q_2 \ q_3] = \begin{bmatrix} q_1q_1 & q_1q_2 & q_1q_3 \\ q_2q_1 & q_2q_2 & q_2q_3 \\ q_3q_1 & q_3q_2 & q_3q_3 \end{bmatrix}$$

and

$$Q = E(qq') = \begin{bmatrix} E(q_1q_1) & E(q_1q_2) & E(q_1q_3) \\ E(q_2q_1) & E(q_2q_2) & E(q_2q_3) \\ E(q_3q_1) & E(q_3q_2) & E(q_3q_3) \end{bmatrix}$$

$$= \begin{bmatrix} q_{11} & q_{12} & q_{13} \\ q_{21} & q_{22} & q_{23} \\ q_{31} & q_{32} & q_{33} \end{bmatrix} \qquad [2.5]$$

Thus, the $(i,j)^{th}$ element of Q, q_{ij}, is the expected value of the product of q_i and q_j.

Since it was assumed that the q_i's are measured as deviations from their means, $q_{ij} = \text{COV}(q_i,q_j)$ and $q_{ii} = \text{COV}(q_i,q_i) = \text{VAR}(q_i)$. Accordingly,

$$Q = \begin{bmatrix} \text{VAR}(q_1) & \text{COV}(q_1,q_2) & \text{COV}(q_1,q_3) \\ \text{COV}(q_2,q_1) & \text{VAR}(q_2) & \text{COV}(q_2,q_3) \\ \text{COV}(q_3,q_1) & \text{COV}(q_3,q_2) & \text{VAR}(q_3) \end{bmatrix}$$

Since the covariance of x_i and x_j is equivalent to the covariance if x_j and x_i, $q_{ij} = q_{ji}$ and Q is a symmetric matrix (i.e., $Q = Q'$). Matrices such as Q are called variance/covariance matrices, or simply covariance matrices.

A number of definitions and assumptions can now be stated. These and other results are summarized in Table 2.1. The population covariance matrix for the observed variables contained in x is defined as $\Sigma = E(xx')$, a $(q \times q)$ symmetric matrix. The $(i,j)^{\text{th}}$ element of Σ, σ_{ij}, is the population value of the covariance between x_i and x_j, and can be defined as $\sigma_{ij} = E(x_i x_j)$. If the x's were standardized to have a variance of one, $E(x_i x_j)$ would be the correlation between x_i and x_j, and Σ would be the population correlation matrix.

The covariances among the common factors are contained in Φ, an $(s \times s)$ symmetric matrix. An individual element of Φ, say ϕ_{ij}, is the covariance between the latent variables ξ_i and ξ_j. Since the factors have zero expectations, $\phi_{ij} = E(\xi_i \xi_j)$ or $\Phi = E(\xi\xi')$. If one assumed that the common factors were uncorrelated, the off-diagonal elements of Φ would be restricted to zeros. If each of the common factors was standardized with a unit variance, Φ would be a correlation matrix with ones on the diagonal and correlations between common factors on the off-diagonals.

The covariances among the residual factors are contained in the population matrix Θ, a $(q \times q)$ symmetric matrix. The $(i,j)^{\text{th}}$ element of Θ, θ_{ij}, is the covariance between unique factors δ_i and δ_j. The unique factors are assumed to have means of zero, in the same way that the errors in equations in regression analysis are assumed to have means of zero. It follows that $\theta_{ij} = E(\delta_i \delta_j)$, or in matrix notation, that $\Theta = E(\delta\delta')$. In most treatments of both the exploratory factor model and the confirmatory factor model, all off-diagonal elements of Θ are assumed to be zero, indicating that the unique factor δ_i affecting the observed variable

TABLE 2.1
Summary of the Confirmatory Factor Model

Matrix	Dimension	Mean	Covariance	Dimension	Description
ξ	$(s \times 1)$	0	$\Phi = E(\xi\xi')$	$(s \times s)$	common factors
x	$(q \times 1)$	0	$\Sigma = E(xx')$	$(q \times q)$	observed variables
Λ	$(q \times s)$	—	—	—	loadings of x on ξ
δ	$(q \times 1)$	0	$\Theta = E(\delta\delta')$	$(q \times q)$	unique factors

Factor Equation: $\quad x = \Lambda\xi + \delta$ [2.4]

Covariance Equation: $\quad \Sigma = \Lambda\Phi\Lambda' + \Theta$ [2.11]

Assumptions:

a. Variables are measured from their means: $E(\xi) = 0$; $E(x) = E(\delta) = 0$.
b. The number of observed variables is greater than the number of common factors; i.e., $q > s$.
c. Common factors and unique factors are uncorrelated: $E(\xi\delta') = 0$ or $E(\delta\xi') = 0$.

x_i is uncorrelated with the unique factor δ_j affecting x_j (for all $i \neq j$). In our treatment of the confirmatory factor model, off-diagonal elements of Θ need not be constrained to equal zero. This allows the unique factor affecting one observed variable to be correlated with the unique factor affecting some other observed variable.[7] Allowing correlated errors is particularly useful in test/retest models and panel models.

While the common factors are allowed to be correlated among themselves and the unique factors are allowed to be correlated among themselves, it is assumed that all common factors are uncorrelated with all unique factors. Mathematically this can be expressed as $E(\xi_i\delta_j) = 0$ for all ξ_i and δ_j. In matrix algebra this assumption can be expressed as $E(\xi\delta') = 0$, or equivalently, $E(\delta\xi') = 0$.

To illustrate the structure and assumptions of the confirmatory factor model, Example 1 is presented again—this time in matrix notation—and a second example is introduced. These examples are extended in later chapters to illustrate the ideas of identification, estimation, and hypothesis testing.

Example 1: a formal specification. The model for the measurement of psychological disorders is reproduced in Figure 2.2. The relationships

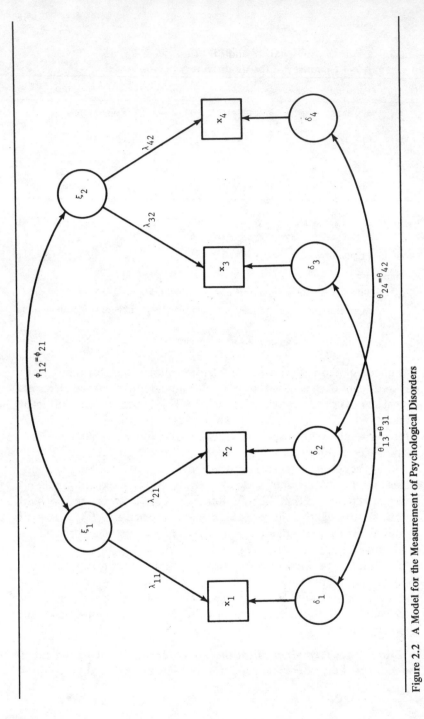

Figure 2.2 A Model for the Measurement of Psychological Disorders

among the observed variables and the common and unique factors were presented in equation 2.3. To translate this equation into a form compatible with the matrix formulation in equation 2.4, it is useful to write the factor equations thus:

$$x_1 = \lambda_{11}\xi_1 + \underline{0}\xi_2 + \delta_1 \qquad [2.6a]$$

$$x_2 = \lambda_{21}\xi_1 + \underline{0}\xi_2 + \delta_2 \qquad [2.6b]$$

$$x_3 = \underline{0}\xi_1 + \lambda_{32}\xi_2 + \delta_3 \qquad [2.6c]$$

$$x_4 = \underline{0}\xi_1 + \lambda_{42}\xi_2 + \delta_4 \qquad [2.6d]$$

which can be written in matrix form as:

$$
\begin{bmatrix} x_1 \\ x_2 \\ x_3 \\ x_4 \end{bmatrix}
=
\begin{bmatrix} \lambda_{11} & \underline{0} \\ \lambda_{21} & \underline{0} \\ \underline{0} & \lambda_{32} \\ \underline{0} & \lambda_{42} \end{bmatrix}
\begin{bmatrix} \xi_1 \\ \xi_2 \end{bmatrix}
+
\begin{bmatrix} \delta_1 \\ \delta_2 \\ \delta_3 \\ \delta_4 \end{bmatrix}
\qquad [2.7]
$$

(Here, and in later chapters, parameters are underlined if they have been constrained to equal the given value.) The reader is encouraged to carry out the necessary matrix operations to reconstruct equation 2.6 from equation 2.7.

Consider equation 2.6a, predicting the observed variable x_1: $x_1 = \lambda_{11}\xi_1 + \underline{0}\xi_2 + \delta_1$. x_1 is defined as a linear combination of the latent variables ξ_1, ξ_2, and δ_1. The coefficient for ξ_1 is λ_{11}, indicating that a unit change in the latent variable ξ_1 results in an average change in x_1 of λ_{11} units. The coefficient for ξ_2 is fixed as zero, indicating that changes in ξ_2 do not directly cause changes in x_1.

In examining the equations 2.6a to 2.6d, one sees that each observed variable loads on only one common factor, with loadings on the other common factors being constrained to zero. In the confirmatory factor model it is up to the researcher to determine which loadings are to be estimated and which are to be constrained to some fixed value. For example, if it made substantive sense to do so, the loading of x_1 on ξ_2 could be freed and the parameter λ_{12} would be estimated.

Each observed variable x_i is also affected by a single residual or unique factor δ_i. The factor δ_i is residual in the sense that it corresponds to that portion of the observed variable x_i that is *not* explained by one or more common factors. Such residual factors are often thought of as random measurement error, unique to each observed variable. Accordingly, they are generally given little substantive consideration.

The curved arrows in the Figure 2.2 correspond to covariances among factors. The arrow connecting ξ_1 and ξ_2 represents the covariance between ξ_1 and ξ_2, which is labeled $\phi_{12} = \phi_{21}$ in Φ:

$$\Phi = \begin{bmatrix} \phi_{11} & \phi_{12} \\ \phi_{21} & \phi_{22} \end{bmatrix} \qquad [2.8]$$

The diagonal elements of Φ are the variances of the common factors, and as such define the scale of these unmeasured variables. The importance of the scale of a latent variable is discussed in Chapter 3.

The variances and covariances among the residual factors are contained in Θ:

$$\Theta = \begin{bmatrix} \theta_{11} & 0 & \theta_{13} & 0 \\ 0 & \theta_{22} & 0 & \theta_{24} \\ \theta_{31} & 0 & \theta_{33} & 0 \\ 0 & \theta_{42} & 0 & \theta_{44} \end{bmatrix} \qquad [2.9]$$

The diagonal elements correspond to the variances of the unique factors. The off-diagonal elements indicate a covariance between the unique factor in the equation explaining one observed variable and the unique factor in the equation explaining another observed variable. Thus, the curved arrow between δ_2 and δ_4 in Figure 2.2, designated by the coefficient ϕ_{24}, indicates that the unique factor δ_2 in the equation 2.6b explaining x_2 and the unique factor δ_4 in equation 2.6d explaining

x_4 are correlated. In this particular example, x_2 and x_4 are variables measured with the same instrument at two points in time. Accordingly, it is likely that their errors in measurement (i.e., unique factors) would be correlated. Covariances between unique factors associated with observed variables that have been measured by different methods have been restricted to zero, as indicated by 0's in equation 2.9.

The assumption that the unique and common factors are uncorrelated (i.e., $E(\xi\delta') = 0$) is represented by the *lack* of curved arrows between the ξ's and δ's in Figure 2.2 //

In Example 1 each observed variable was affected (i.e., loaded on) by only one common factor. In many applications it is reasonable to assume that an observed variable loads on more than one factor. This is the case in the multimethod-multitrait (MMMT) model. In the MMMT model each of a set of traits is measured by each of a set of methods. If the measurement of a trait is not affected by the method used in measurement, the observed variable would load on only the common factor for that trait, and not on the common factor for that method. However, if there is an effect of the method of measurement, then each observed variable would load on both the factor for that particular trait and the factor for the particular method used. The MMMT model attempts to disentangle the effects of different substantive concepts from the methods of measurement used to measure those concepts. This model can be easily formulated as a confirmatory factor model, as our next example illustrates. For more details on the MMMT model, see Alwin (1974); Kenny (1979); and Sullivan and Feldman (1979).

Example 2: the multimethod-multitrait model. Consider a study in which three traits are being measured with each of three methods. Let the three traits correspond to the trait factors ξ_1, ξ_2, and ξ_3, and let the three methods correspond to the method factors ξ_4, ξ_5, and ξ_6. There are nine observed variables: x_1 to x_3 are measures of traits ξ_1 to ξ_3 by method ξ_4; x_4 to x_6 are measures of traits ξ_1 to ξ_3 by method ξ_5; and x_7 to x_9 are measures of traits ξ_1 to ξ_3 by method ξ_6.

Figure 2.3 shows the loadings of the observed variables on the factors. A given method factor is assumed to affect only those observed variables measured by that method. For example, since x_1 to x_3 are all measured by method ξ_4, they load on ξ_4 but not ξ_5 and ξ_6. Similarly, a given trait factor is assumed to affect only those observed variables that are measures of that trait. For example, x_1, x_4, and x_7 are measures of trait ξ_1 by each of the methods and load on the trait factor ξ_1, but not on

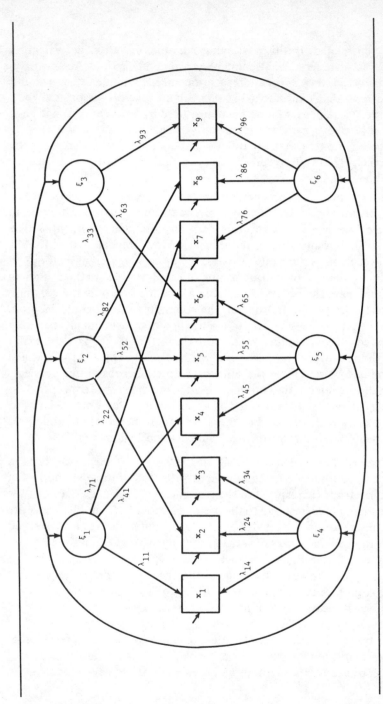

30

Figure 2.3 A Multimethod-Multitrait Model

the trait factors ξ_2 and ξ_3. This information is contained in the loading matrix Λ:

$$
\Lambda =
\begin{array}{c}
\overbrace{\hspace{6em}}^{\text{Trait Loadings}} \quad \overbrace{\hspace{6em}}^{\text{Method Loadings}}
\end{array}
$$

$\Lambda =$	λ_{11}	$\underline{0}$	$\underline{0}$	λ_{14}	$\underline{0}$	$\underline{0}$	x_1
	$\underline{0}$	λ_{22}	$\underline{0}$	λ_{24}	$\underline{0}$	$\underline{0}$	x_2
	$\underline{0}$	$\underline{0}$	λ_{33}	λ_{34}	$\underline{0}$	$\underline{0}$	x_3
	λ_{41}	$\underline{0}$	$\underline{0}$	$\underline{0}$	λ_{45}	$\underline{0}$	x_4
	$\underline{0}$	λ_{52}	$\underline{0}$	$\underline{0}$	λ_{55}	$\underline{0}$	x_5
	$\underline{0}$	$\underline{0}$	λ_{63}	$\underline{0}$	λ_{65}	$\underline{0}$	x_6
	λ_{71}	$\underline{0}$	$\underline{0}$	$\underline{0}$	$\underline{0}$	λ_{76}	x_7
	$\underline{0}$	λ_{82}	$\underline{0}$	$\underline{0}$	$\underline{0}$	λ_{86}	x_8
	$\underline{0}$	$\underline{0}$	λ_{93}	$\underline{0}$	$\underline{0}$	λ_{96}	x_9
	ξ_1	ξ_2	ξ_3	ξ_{44}	ξ_5	ξ_6	

The x's and ξ's are added as borders to indicate which observed variables and common factors are being linked by a particular loading.

Covariances among latent variables are contained in Φ, a (6×6) symmetric matrix. These covariances are indicated by the continuous curve connecting all common factors in Figure 2.3. This matrix contains covariances among trait factors, covariances among method factors, and covariances between trait factors and method factors. If all factors are assumed to be correlated, we have

$$
\Phi = \left[\begin{array}{ccc|ccc}
\phi_{11} & \phi_{12} & \phi_{13} & \phi_{14} & \phi_{15} & \phi_{16} \\
\phi_{21} & \phi_{22} & \phi_{23} & \phi_{24} & \phi_{25} & \phi_{26} \\
\phi_{31} & \phi_{32} & \phi_{33} & \phi_{34} & \phi_{35} & \phi_{36} \\
\hline
\phi_{41} & \phi_{42} & \phi_{43} & \phi_{44} & \phi_{45} & \phi_{46} \\
\phi_{51} & \phi_{52} & \phi_{53} & \phi_{54} & \phi_{55} & \phi_{56} \\
\phi_{61} & \phi_{62} & \phi_{63} & \phi_{64} & \phi_{65} & \phi_{66}
\end{array} \right]
= \left[\begin{array}{c|c}
\text{trait/} & \text{trait/} \\
\text{trait} & \text{method} \\
\hline
\text{method/} & \text{method/} \\
\text{trait} & \text{method}
\end{array} \right]
$$

The trait/trait block contains covariances among the trait factors. To understand these covariances it is useful to contrast them with the covariances among the observed variables. For example, σ_{12} is the covariance between the observed variable x_1, which measures trait ξ_1 with method ξ_4, and x_2, which measures trait ξ_2 with the same method. Ideally we would like to know the covariance between the traits ξ_1 and ξ_2, uncontaminated by the effects of the method of measurement used. Even though σ_{12} reflects this covariance, it also reflects the variance in the method factor ξ_4 (ϕ_{44}), the covariances between the trait factors ξ_1 and ξ_2 and the method factor ξ_4 (ϕ_{14} and ϕ_{24}), and the loadings of the x_1 and x_2 on the factors $\xi_1, \xi_2,$ and ξ_4 ($\lambda_{11}, \lambda_{14}, \lambda_{22},$ and λ_{24}). This can be seen by multiplying the factor equation $x_1 = \lambda_{11}\xi_1 + \lambda_{14}\xi_4 + \delta_1$ by the factor equation $x_2 = \lambda_{22}\xi_2 + \lambda_{24}\xi_4 + \delta_2$ and taking expectations

$$
E(x_1 x_2) = \lambda_{11}\lambda_{22}E(\xi_1\xi_2) + \lambda_{14}\lambda_{22}E(\xi_2\xi_4) + \lambda_{22}E(\xi_2\delta_1)
$$

$$
+ \lambda_{11}\lambda_{24}E(\xi_1\xi_4) + \lambda_{14}\lambda_{24}E(\xi_4\xi_4) + \lambda_{24}E(\xi_4\delta_2)
$$

$$
+ \lambda_{11}E(\xi_1\delta_2) + \lambda_{14}E(\xi_4\delta_2) + E(\delta_1\delta_2)
$$

Since ξ_1, ξ_2, and ξ_4 are assumed to be uncorrelated with δ_1 and δ_2, and δ_1 and δ_2 are assumed to be uncorrelated, it follows that

$$\sigma_{12} = \lambda_{11}\lambda_{22}\phi_{12} + \lambda_{14}\lambda_{22}\phi_{24} + \lambda_{11}\lambda_{24}\phi_{14} + \lambda_{14}\lambda_{24}\phi_{44}$$

The factors contaminating the covariances between observed variables are eliminated by the trait/trait covariance in Φ. Indeed, a primary motivation in applying the MMMT model is to estimate covariances (or correlations) among traits that are unaffected by method.

Variances and covariance among the unique factors are contained in Θ. In the MMMT model the unique factors are usually assumed to be uncorrelated. The unique factors are represented by the unlabeled arrows in Figure 2.3 //

The Covariance Structure

In these examples the relationships among the observed variables and the latent variables have been specified in a manner similar to multiple regression analysis. One important difference exists, however. While the dependent variables are observed in both regression analysis and factor analysis, the independent variables are unobserved in factor models. Consequently, the parameters of the model cannot be directly estimated by regressing the dependent x's on the independent ξ's.

Since the factor equation 2.4 cannot be directly estimated, it is necessary to examine the structure of the covariances among the observed variables (contained in the matrix Σ) in terms of the structure implied by the right-hand side of equation 2.4. This is accomplished by multiplying equation 2.4 by its transpose and taking expectations

$$\Sigma = E(xx') = E[(\Lambda\xi + \delta)(\Lambda\xi + \delta)']$$

Since the transpose of a sum of matrices is equal to the sum of the transpose of the matrices, and the transpose of a product of matrices is the product of the transposes in reverse order, it follows that

$$\Sigma = E[(\Lambda\xi + \delta)(\xi'\Lambda' + \delta')]$$

Using the distributive property for matrices and taking expectations

$$\Sigma = E[\Lambda\xi\xi'\Lambda' + \Lambda\xi\delta' + \delta\xi'\Lambda' + \delta\delta']$$

$$= E[\Lambda\xi\xi'\Lambda'] + E[\Lambda\xi\delta'] + E[\delta\xi'\Lambda'] + E[\delta\delta']$$

The parameter matrix Λ does not contain random variables, since the population values of the parameters are constant (even if unknown). This allows us to write

$$\Sigma = \Lambda E[\xi\xi']\Lambda' + \Lambda E[\xi\delta'] + E[\delta\xi']\Lambda' + E[\delta\delta'] \qquad [2.10]$$

Finally, since $E[\xi\xi']$ is defined as Φ, $E[\delta\delta']$ is defined as Θ, and δ and ξ are assumed to be uncorrelated, equation 2.10 can be simplified to:

$$\Sigma = \Lambda\Phi\Lambda' + \Theta \qquad [2.11]$$

This important equation is referred to as the *covariance equation*.

While some readers may not follow the matrix manipulations in the last derivation, it is important to understand what has been accomplished. The left side of the equation contains $q(q + 1)/2$ distinct variances and covariances among the observed variables.[8] The right side of the equation contains qs possible loadings from Λ, $s(s + 1)/2$ independent variances and covariances among the ξ's; and $q(q + 1)/2$ independent variances and covariances among the δ's. Thus, equation 2.11 decomposes the $q(q + 1)/2$ distinct elements of Σ into $[qs + s(s + 1)/2 + q(q + 1)/2]$ unknown, independent parameters from the matrices Λ, Φ, and Θ. The unknown parameters that are to be estimated have been tied to the population variances and covariances among the observed variables. Unlike the parameters in Λ, Φ, and Θ, these variances and covariances can be directly estimated with sample data. It is this link that makes estimation possible. Before estimation can proceed, however, it is necessary to determine whether it is possible to obtain unique estimates of the parameters. This is the problem of *identification*.

3. IDENTIFICATION OF THE CONFIRMATORY FACTOR MODEL

Estimation and Identification

While justification for estimating the parameters is contingent upon the identification of the model, identification and estimation are distinct issues (see, for example, Wonnacott and Wonnacott, 1979: 276). Estimation involves using *sample* data to make estimates of *population* parameters. In the confirmatory factor model this involves using the sample matrix of covariances, called **S**, to estimate the parameters in Λ, Φ, and Θ. Concern is with such issues as bias (are the estimates on average equal to the true parameters?) and efficiency (are the sample data being used in the most effective way?). Identification is concerned with whether the parameters of the model are *uniquely* determined. If a model is not identified, it is impossible to uniquely determine the parameters even if the values for each observed variable are known for the entire population. In the confirmatory factor model this means that even if the population covariance matrix Σ were known (i.e., did not have to be estimated with a sample matrix **S**), it would be impossible to uniquely solve the covariance equation $\Sigma = \Lambda\Phi\Lambda' + \Theta$ for the parameters in Λ, Φ, and Θ. If the model were not identified, it would be possible to find an infinite number of values for the parameters, each set of which would be consistent with the covariance equation.

Estimation assumes that the model is identified. Sample data contained in **S** and information about the structure of the model (i.e., knowledge about the constraints on the parameters that are to be estimated) is used to find estimates $\hat{\Lambda}$, $\hat{\Phi}$, and $\hat{\Theta}$ of the population parameters. These estimates result in predictions of the population variances and covariances of the observed variables according to the equation $\hat{\Sigma} = \hat{\Lambda}\hat{\Phi}\hat{\Lambda}' + \hat{\Theta}$. The problem of estimation is finding $\hat{\Lambda}$, $\hat{\Phi}$, and $\hat{\Theta}$ such that the predicted covariance matrix $\hat{\Sigma}$ is as close as possible to the observed variances and covariances contained in **S**. How this is accomplished and what is meant by "as close as possible" is the subject of Chapter 4. For now, this is the critical issue relating identification and estimation: *Attempts to estimate models that are not identified result in arbitrary estimates of the parameters and meaningless interpretations.* Note well that computer programs will estimate identified as well as unidentified models, providing useful information in the case of identified models and useless information in the case of unidentified models. Identification *must* be established before estimation proceeds.

Identification is not an issue unique to the confirmatory factor model. For example, identification is an important issue in simultaneous equation models and exploratory factor models. One important practical difference exists between identification in the confirmatory factor model and these other models. For simultaneous equation models and exploratory factor models there are rules that can be routinely applied to a large class of commonly encountered models. For simultaneous equation models these are the well-known rank and order conditions (see, for example, Wonnacott and Wonnacott, 1979); for the exploratory factor model these are rules on the number of parameters relative to the number of variances and covariances among observed variables (see, for example, Lawley and Maxwell, 1971). For the confirmatory factor model the rules that are avaiable apply to only a limited number of special cases. Consequently, proving that a model is identified presents one of the greatest practical difficulties in using the confirmatory factor model.

Identification

To understand why identification is a problem, it is useful to recast the problem as follows. Consider the factor model presented in equation 3.1:

$$\mathbf{x} = \Lambda \xi + \delta \qquad [3.1]$$

As shown in Chapter 2, this model implies that the variances and covariances of the observed variables and the parameters Λ, Φ, and θ are related according to the covariance equation

$$\Sigma = \Lambda \Phi \Lambda' + \Theta \qquad [3.2]$$

Unless restrictions are imposed on the parameters in Λ, Φ, and Θ, if there is one set of parameters that satisfies equation 3.2, there will be an infinite number of such sets. To see why this is so, let $\mathbf{M}$ be any (s × s) invertible matrix.[9] If we define $\ddot{\Lambda} = \Lambda \mathbf{M}^{-1}$; $\ddot{\xi} = \mathbf{M}\xi$; and $\ddot{\Phi} = \mathbf{M}\Phi\mathbf{M}'$, both the Λ, Φ, and Θ matrices, and the $\ddot{\Lambda}$, $\ddot{\Phi}$, and $\ddot{\Theta}$ matrices satisfy equations 3.1 and 3.4. This can be easily demonstrated.

$$\ddot{\Lambda} \ddot{\xi} + \delta = (\Lambda \mathbf{M}^{-1})(\mathbf{M}\xi) + \delta$$

$$= \Lambda (\mathbf{M}^{-1}\mathbf{M})\xi + \delta$$

$$= \Lambda \xi + \delta \qquad [3.3]$$

Thus, if $\mathbf{x} = \Lambda \xi + \delta$, it is also true that $\mathbf{x} = \ddot{\Lambda} \ddot{\xi} + \delta$. Applying the same procedures to the covariance equation 3.2,

$$\ddot{\Lambda} \ddot{\Phi} \ddot{\Lambda}' + \Theta = (\Lambda M^{-1})(M\Phi M')(M'^{-1}\Lambda') + \Theta$$

$$= \Lambda(MM^{-1})\Phi(M'M'^{-1})\Lambda' + \Theta$$

$$= \Lambda\Phi\Lambda' + \Theta = \Sigma \qquad\qquad [3.4]$$

Thus, if $\Sigma = \Lambda\Phi\Lambda' + \Theta$, it is also true that $\Sigma = \ddot{\Lambda}\ddot{\Phi}\ddot{\Lambda}' + \Theta$. Since the "``''" matrices do not equal the original matrices unless $M = I$, each of the infinite number of invertible M matrices provides an *equally satisfactory* solution to the model. That is, the model is unidentified.

Example 1: the covariance structure. To illustrate this idea, consider the model from Wheaton (1978). Assume, for purposes of demonstration, that the population covariance matrix for the four observed variables is

$$\Sigma = \begin{bmatrix} 0.50 & 0.16 & 0.12 & 0.08 \\ 0.16 & 1.00 & 0.12 & 0.20 \\ 0.12 & 0.12 & 1.60 & 1.44 \\ 0.08 & 0.20 & 1.44 & 2.00 \end{bmatrix}$$

Assume that the population parameter matrices Λ, Φ, and Θ are unknown except that they must reproduce the population covariance matrix Σ given above when substituted into this equation $\Sigma = \Lambda\Phi\Lambda' + \Theta$.

Consider the matrices $\Lambda^{(1)}$, $\Phi^{(1)}$, and $\Theta^{(1)}$ as possibilities for the population parameters. If they are defined as

$$\Lambda^{(1)} = \begin{bmatrix} 0.20 & 0.00 \\ 0.40 & 0.00 \\ 0.00 & 0.60 \\ 0.00 & 0.80 \end{bmatrix} \qquad \Phi^{(1)} = \begin{bmatrix} 2.00 & 0.50 \\ 0.50 & 3.00 \end{bmatrix}$$

and

$$\boldsymbol{\Theta}^{(1)} = \begin{bmatrix} 0.42 & 0.00 & 0.06 & 0.00 \\ 0.00 & 0.68 & 0.00 & 0.04 \\ 0.06 & 0.00 & 0.52 & 0.00 \\ 0.00 & 0.04 & 0.00 & 0.08 \end{bmatrix}$$

then the equality $\boldsymbol{\Sigma} = \boldsymbol{\Lambda}^{(1)}\boldsymbol{\Phi}^{(1)}\boldsymbol{\Lambda}^{(1)\prime} + \boldsymbol{\Theta}^{(1)}$ holds. (The reader is encouraged to carry out the necessary matrix operations to verify this statement.) Thus, the $10 = [q(q + 1)/2]$ independent elements of $\boldsymbol{\Sigma}$ are decomposed into—hence are reproduced by—the $21 = qs + [s(s + 1)/2] + [q(q + 1)/2]$ independent elements of the matrices $\boldsymbol{\Lambda}^{(1)}$, $\boldsymbol{\Phi}^{(1)}$, and $\boldsymbol{\Theta}^{(1)}$. The "(1)" matrices satisfy the conditions required of the true parameter matrices: They are of correct dimension and they reproduce the population covariance matrix. The only remaining question is, are they unique, or are there other matrices of correct dimension that also reproduce the population covariance matrix? That is, is the model identified?

To illustrate why the model as currently stated is not identified, let $\mathbf{M}^{(1)}$ and $\mathbf{M}^{(1)^{-1}}$ be defined as

$$\mathbf{M}^{(1)} = \begin{bmatrix} -1.0 & 1.0 \\ 2.0 & -3.0 \end{bmatrix}$$

and

$$\mathbf{M}^{(1)^{-1}} = \begin{bmatrix} -3.0 & -1.0 \\ -2.0 & -1.0 \end{bmatrix}$$

New Λ and Φ matrices can be formed by carrying out the following matrix multiplications on the first set of parameter matrices:

$$\Lambda^{(2)} = \Lambda^{(1)}M^{(1)^{-1}} = \begin{bmatrix} -0.60 & -0.20 \\ -1.20 & -0.40 \\ -1.20 & -0.60 \\ -1.60 & -0.80 \end{bmatrix}$$

and

$$\Phi^{(2)} = M^{(1)}\Phi^{(1)}M^{(1)\prime} = \begin{bmatrix} 4.0 & -10.5 \\ -10.5 & 29.0 \end{bmatrix}$$

with $\Theta^{(1)}$ remaining unchanged. These new parameter matrices have the same dimensions as the first set of matrices, which satisfies the first requirement. Substituting the "(2)" parameters into the covariance equation reproduces the population covariance matrix Σ. That is, $\Sigma = \Lambda^{(2)}\Phi^{(2)}\Lambda^{(2)\prime} + \Theta^{(1)}$. Hence, the second requirement is satisfied. (Once again, the reader should verify this fact.) Since both sets of parameter matrices reproduce Σ, they can both be thought of as solutions to the covariance equation.

While both solutions are acceptable in terms of reproducing the covariance matrix, each suggests a different structure. In $\Lambda^{(1)}$ each observed variable loads on only one common factor, while in $\Lambda^{(2)}$ each observed variable loads on both common factors. In $\Phi^{(1)}$ the common factors are positively correlated, while in $\Phi^{(2)}$ they are negatively correlated. Since both sets of parameters are equally acceptable in terms of reproducing the covariances among observed variables, any interpretation of the parameters is misleading.

To distinguish between the two sets of potential parameters, additional criteria must be used. Recall that in originally describing the model (see Figure 2.2) it was argued that each observed variable should load on only one common factor (i.e., $\lambda_{12} = \lambda_{22} = \lambda_{31} = \lambda_{41} = 0$). With respect to these substantively motivated constraints on the λ's, the (1) solution would be acceptable, while the (2) solution would not. Thus, by imposing constraints on some of the loadings, at least one possible set of parameters is eliminated. The model is identified if the first solution set is the only set of parameters that can reproduce the variances and covariances among the observed variables and maintain the imposed constraints. Whether or not this is the case is considered below.//

Our example illustrates that the factor model is not identified if there are no constraints imposed on the parameters. Without constraints an indeterminacy exists, which allows more than one set of acceptable parameter values. In the exploratory factor model this indeterminacy is often eliminated by imposing the constraint that $\Lambda'\Theta^{-1}\Lambda$ is a diagonal matrix whose elements are distinct, positive, and arranged in descending order (Lawley and Maxwell, 1971: 8).[10] The model is identified since the diagonality constraint eliminates all but one set of possible parameters. The problem is that the constraint is substantively arbitrary. In the confirmatory factor model identification is achieved by imposing constraints based on substantive considerations. Examples of the types of constraints that can be imposed illustrate the advantage of this approach.

Fixing an element of Λ, say λ_{ij}, to zero means that the observed variable x_i is not causally affected by the common factor ξ_j; that is, x_i does not load on ξ_j. Fixing an element of Φ, say ϕ_{ij} where $i \neq j$, to zero means that the common factors ξ_i and ξ_j are uncorrelated. If all off-diagonal elements of Φ are zero ($\phi_{ij} = 0$ for all $i \neq j$), the factor structure is said to be orthogonal. Since Φ is symmetric, fixing $\phi_{ij} = 0$ implies that $\phi_{ji} = 0$; hence only one independent constraint is being imposed. If diagonal elements of Φ are set to zero, say $\phi_{ii} = 0$, the common factor is in effect eliminated, since it has no variation. Similar constraints can be imposed on Θ. If $\theta_{ij} = 0$ for $i \neq j$, then the unique factor affecting x_i is independent of the unique factor affecting x_j. Setting $\theta_{ii} = 0$ indicates that x_i is perfectly determined by the common factors of the model, with no unique component.

Equality constraints can also be imposed. For example, if there are multiple measurements of an underlying factor one might assume that $\lambda_{1j} = \lambda_{2j} = \ldots = \lambda_{qj}$, meaning that all indicators depend on the underlying factor ξ_j in the same way. With equality constraints the value of the parameters constrained to be equal is unknown. Thus, if four parameters are constrained to be equal, only three independent constraints are being imposed, since the value to which they are all equal is unknown.

The confirmatory factor model is identified if the constraints have been imposed in such a way that there is a unique set of parameters that generate Σ according to the covariance equation 3.2. The constraints on parameters in the confirmatory factor model have the same effect as the diagonalization assumption in the exploratory factor model. The major difference is that in the exploratory factor model the diagonalization assumption *always* eliminates all but one set of values for the parameters; hence the model is known to be identified (even if the imposed constraints are substantively meaningless). In the confirmatory factor model the user cannot readily determine if the imposed constraints eliminate all but one set of values for the parameters; hence identification must be proven individually for each model. Example 1 illustrates this point.

Example 1: identification. When this example was initially described, a set of constraints was imposed on Λ. It was assumed that $\lambda_{12} = \lambda_{22} = \lambda_{31} = \lambda_{41} = 0$; that is, x_1 and x_2 load only on ξ_1, while x_3 and x_4 load only on ξ_2. The loading matrix $\Lambda^{(1)}$, defined above, retains these constraints, but $\Lambda^{(2)}$ does not. Thus, the constraints imposed on Λ eliminated at least one possible loading matrix. Nonetheless, the constraints imposed on the loadings are not sufficient to identify the model. This can be seen by considering the matrix $\mathbf{M}^{(3)}$, a diagonal matrix with 1.0 as the $(1,1)^{th}$ element and 2.0 as the $(2,2)^{th}$ element. With this matrix another set of Λ and Φ matrices can be constructed that both reproduces the covariance matrix Σ (as did the matrices constructed with $\mathbf{M}^{(1)}$) and maintains the imposed constraints (as $\Lambda^{(2)}$ did not). These new matrices are

$$\Lambda^{(3)} = \Lambda^{(1)} \mathbf{M}^{(3)^{-1}} = \begin{bmatrix} 0.2 & 0.0 \\ 0.4 & 0.0 \\ 0.0 & 0.3 \\ 0.0 & 0.4 \end{bmatrix}$$

and

$$\Phi^{(3)} = M^{(3)}\Phi^{(1)}M^{(3)\prime} = \begin{bmatrix} 2.0 & 1.0 \\ 1.0 & 12.0 \end{bmatrix}$$

The reader should verify that $\Sigma = \Lambda^{(3)}\Phi^{(3)}\Lambda^{(3)\prime} + \Theta^{(1)}$, where Σ and $\Theta^{(1)}$ are defined in our earlier example. Thus, while some parameter matrices can be eliminated by the constraints on Λ, not all can. Once again it must be concluded that the model is not identified. //

Conditions for Identification

While it is known that imposing constraints will eliminate at least some possible solutions to the factor model, what is required is a set of easily verifiable conditions that determine unambiguously whether a model is identified. Such conditions are of three types: (1) necessary conditions, which if *not* satisfied indicate that a model is not identified, but if satisfied do not necessarily mean that the model is identified; (2) sufficient conditions, which if met imply that the model is identified, but if not met do not imply that the model is unidentified (although it may be that it is unidentified); and (3) necessary and sufficient conditions, which if satisfied imply that the model is identified, and if not satisfied imply that the model is not identified.

The simplest necessary condition relates the number of independent covariance equations to the number of independent, unconstrained parameters. Covariance equation 3.2 contains $q(q + 1)/2$ independent equations, one for each of the independent elements of the $(q \times q)$ symmetric matrix Σ. If there are more independent parameters than covariance equations, there will be many solutions to equation 3.2 and the model will not be identified. Since there are $qs + [s(s + 1)/2] + [q(q + 1)/2]$ possible independent parameters in Λ, Φ, and Θ, a confirmatory factor model is unidentified unless *at least* $qs + [s(s + 1)/2]$ constraints are imposed. Hence, a necessary but not sufficient condition for identification is that the number of independent, unconstrained parameters in the model must be less than or equal to $q(q + 1)/2$. This condition is easy to apply, as is now illustrated.

Example 1: testing a necessary condition for identification. In this example there are four observed variables and thus, 10 $[= 4(4 + 1)/2]$ distinct variances and covariances in Σ. There are thirteen independent parameters. These are numbered in the following matrices; elements marked with * are fixed.

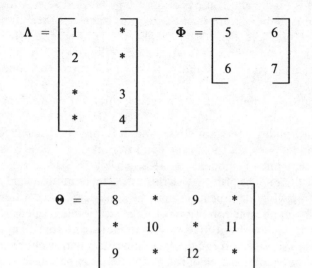

$$\Lambda = \begin{bmatrix} 1 & * \\ 2 & * \\ * & 3 \\ * & 4 \end{bmatrix} \qquad \Phi = \begin{bmatrix} 5 & 6 \\ 6 & 7 \end{bmatrix}$$

and

$$\Theta = \begin{bmatrix} 8 & * & 9 & * \\ * & 10 & * & 11 \\ 9 & * & 12 & * \\ * & 11 & * & 13 \end{bmatrix}$$

Since the number of independent parameters is greater than the number of independent covariance equations (13 > 10), the necessary condition for identification is not satisfied and the model is not identified. If the number of independent parameters had been less than or equal to the number of independent covariance equations, it would not necessarily mean that the model was identified, since the condition is necessary, but not sufficient. //

Jöreskog (1969:186) described what were thought to be two sufficient conditions, originally presented by Howe (1955). First, if $\Phi = I$ and the columns of Λ are arranged such that column k contains at least $(k - 1)$ fixed elements, the model is identified. Second, if Φ is not diagonal but its diagonal elements are ones (i.e., all factors are standardized to have unit variance), the model is identified if there are at least $(s-1)$ fixed elements in each of the columns of Λ. These conditions have been presented and applied frequently (Werts et al., 1973; Bielby and Hauser, 1977; Burt et al., 1978; Long, 1976), but recent research has shown that these conditions are *not* sufficient (Dunn, 1973; Jennrich, 1978; Burt et al., 1979). Jöreskog (1979) has found one sufficient condition that does hold, however. A confirmatory factor model is identified if (1) Φ is a symmetric, positive definite matrix with diagonal elements equal to one;[11] (2) Θ is diagonal; (3) Λ has at least (s − 1) fixed zeros (nonzero fixed elements do not count) in each column, where s is the number of common factors; and (4) Λ^k has rank (s − 1), where Λ^k (for k = 1, 2, . . . s) is the submatrix of Λ consisting of the rows of Λ that have fixed zero elements in the k[th]column.[12] An application of this condition is given below.

This condition is limited in two respects. First, it does not apply to many useful models (e.g., models with fixed values not equal to zero; models with equality constraints). Second, it is only a sufficient condition. If a model does not satisfy the condition, it does not necessarily mean that the model is unidentified. Rather, all that is known is that identification cannot be proven with this sufficient condition, and other methods of proving identification must be considered. Accordingly, a more broadly applicable condition for identification is needed.

In general, the most effective way to demonstrate that a model is identified is to show that through algebraic manipulations of the model's covariance equations each of the parameters can be solved in terms of the population variances and covariances of the observed variables. This is a necessary and sufficient condition for identification. If the condition is satisfied, the model is identified; if the condition is not satisfied, the model is not identified. In the case in which the variables are standardized, as noted by Werts et al. (1973: 1473), solving the equations for the parameters is equivalent to solving the path equations. Duncan (1975) and Kenny (1979) are two useful sources dealing with techniques for solving path equations.

With this approach, parameters are identified on an individual basis. If a parameter can be solved for in terms of the variances and covariances of the observed variables, it is identified. If a parameter can be solved in more than one way, the parameter is overidentified—a special case of being identified. The model as a whole is identified if all of the individual parameters are identified. If a model is identified, but some or all of the parameters are overidentified, the model is said to be overidentified—a special case of being identified. Finally, if the covariance equations cannot be solved for a particular parameter, the parameter is unidentified and the model as a whole is unidentified. Note that individual parameters can be identified when the model as a whole is not identified. These identified parameters can be estimated, even though the unidentified parameters cannot. This point is illustrated below.

In practice, solving the covariance equations can be time-consuming. It is tempting to forgo the task and to assume that the model is identified, as all too many retractions for published findings illustrate. It cannot be emphasized strongly enough that if a model is not identified, estimates of the parameters that are not identified are arbitrary and interpretations are meaningless. *Identification must be established before attempts are made to estimate a model.*

Jöreskog and Sörbom (Jöreskog, 1979; Jöreskog and Sörbom, 1981) have recently argued that the computer can be used to determine identification. In computing maximum likelihood estimates of the parameters (a topic discussed in Chapter 4), the information matrix for the parameters can be computed. (See Kmenta [1971: 174-186] for a technical discussion of the information matrix.) Roughly speaking, the information matrix corresponds to a matrix of variances and covariances for the parameter estimates. Jöreskog and Sörbom (1978:11) stated, "if [the information matrix] is positive definite it is *almost certain* that the model is identified. On the other hand, if the information matrix is singular, the model is not identified" (italics added). The software can check these conditions and indicate whether or not the model appears to be identified. Even though this is a tempting solution to the identification problem, the reader is warned that it is not a necessary and sufficient condition for identification. If the information matrix is positive definite, it is possible, even if unlikely, that the model is not identified. If a user happens to estimate a model for which the "almost certain" condition is satisfied, but the model is not identified, the resulting analyses are meaningless. The emphatic recommendation: Always prove that your model is identified by solving the model's parameters in terms of the variances and covariances of the observed variables.[13] On the other hand, if identification has been "proven" by solving the parameters in terms of the covariances among the observed variables, and the program indicates that the information matrix is *not* positive definite, an error in the proof of identification or in running the program may have been made.

Example 1: identification. To illustrate how identification is proven and what components characterize an unidentified model, a variety of models are considered for the measurement of psychological disorder. To make the presentation easier to follow, Table 3.1 provides a summary of each model that is considered here or later in the text. Figure 3.1

TABLE 3.1
Models Considered in Example 1

Model	λ_{11}	λ_{21}	λ_{32}	λ_{42}	ϕ_{11}	ϕ_{22}	ϕ_{12}	θ_{11}	θ_{22}	θ_{33}	θ_{44}	θ_{13}	θ_{24}
M_a	*	*	*	*	*	*	*	*	*	*	*	0	0
M_b	A	B	A	B	*	*	*	*	*	*	*	0	0
M_c	*	*	*	*	1	1	*	*	*	*	*	0	0
M_d	1	*	1	*	*	*	*	*	*	*	*	0	0
M_e	A	B	A	B	1	1	*	*	*	*	*	0	*
M_f	A	B	A	B	1	1	*	*	*	*	*	*	*
M_g	1	A	1	A	B	B	*	*	*	*	*	0	0
M_h	1	A	1	A	B	B	*	*	*	*	*	0	*

NOTE: * indicates that a parameter is estimated; pairs of capital letters indicate that those parameters have been constrained to be equal; numbers indicate fixed value for a parameter.

illustrates the model with all of the parameters that are to be considered.

Consider model M_a described in Table 3.1. There are eleven parameters (λ_{11}, λ_{21}, λ_{32}, λ_{42}, ϕ_{11}, ϕ_{22}, ϕ_{12}, θ_{11}, θ_{22}, θ_{33}, θ_{44}), but only 10 [= $q(q + 1)/2$] variances and covariances. Therefore, the necessary condition for identification is not satisfied, and M_a is not identified.

In longitudinal models with multiple indicators, such as the current example, it is often reasonable to assume that the factor loadings for a given measure at different points in time are identical. For the current example this involves imposing the equality constraints $\lambda_{11} = \lambda_{32}$ and $\lambda_{21} = \lambda_{42}$. M_b adds these constraints to M_a. By imposing two constraints, two of the original eleven independent parameters have been eliminated, leaving nine. Accordingly, the necessary condition for identification is satisfied, and an attempt can be made to solve the covariance equations for the parameters. To facilitate such a solution it is useful to rewrite the factor equations (equation 2.6 above) incorporating the constraints:

$$x_1 = \lambda_{11}\xi_1 + \delta_1 \qquad x_2 = \lambda_{21}\xi_1 + \delta_2$$

$$x_3 = \lambda_{11}\xi_2 + \delta_3 \qquad x_4 = \lambda_{21}\xi_2 + \delta_4 \qquad [3.5]$$

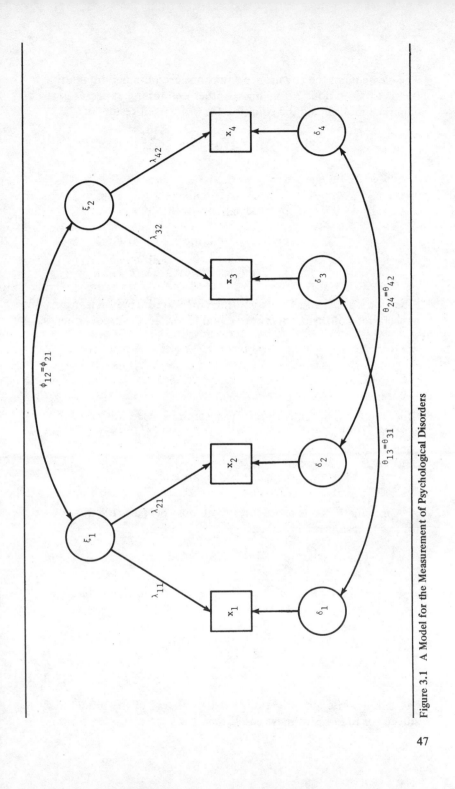

Figure 3.1 A Model for the Measurement of Psychological Disorders

47

The elements of the covariance equations are obtained by multiplying the factor equations 3.5 by one another and taking expectations. For example, multiplying the equation for x_1 by itself results in

$$x_1 x_1 = \lambda_{11}^2 \xi_1 \xi_1 + \delta_1 \delta_1 + 2\lambda_{11}\xi_1\delta_1$$

Taking expectations,

$$E(x_1 x_1) = E(\lambda_{11}^2 \xi_1 \xi_1 + \delta_1 \delta_1 + 2\lambda_{11}\xi_1\delta_1)$$

$$= E(\lambda_{11}^2 \xi_1 \xi_1) + E(\delta_1 \delta_1) + E(2\lambda_{11}\xi_1\delta_1)$$

$$= \lambda_{11}^2 E(\xi_1 \xi_1) + E(\delta_1 \delta_1) + 2\lambda_{11}E(\xi_1\delta_1)$$

Since the x's, ξ's, and δ's are assumed measured from their means, the expectations of the products are equal to variances or covariances.

$$VAR(x_1) = \lambda_{11}^2 VAR(\xi_1) + VAR(\delta_1) + 2\lambda_{11}COV(\xi_1, \delta_1)$$

$$= \lambda_{11}^2 \phi_{11} + \theta_{11} + 0$$

which follows by substituting the symbols used for $VAR(\xi_1)$ and $VAR(\delta_1)$, and using the assumption that $COV(\xi_1, \delta_1)$ is zero. Thus, we conclude that

$$\sigma_{11} = \lambda_{11}^2 \phi_{11} + \theta_{11}$$

Applying the same procedures to all possible pairs of equations, the following results are obtained:

$$\sigma_{11} = \lambda_{11}^2 \phi_{11} + \theta_{11} \qquad\qquad \sigma_{22} = \lambda_{21}^2 \phi_{11} + \theta_{22}$$

$$\sigma_{33} = \lambda_{11}^2 \phi_{22} + \theta_{33} \qquad\qquad \sigma_{44} = \lambda_{21}^2 \phi_{22} + \theta_{44}$$

$$\sigma_{12} = \lambda_{11}\lambda_{21}\phi_{11} \qquad \sigma_{13} = \lambda_{11}^2 \phi_{12} \qquad \sigma_{14} = \lambda_{11}\lambda_{21}\phi_{12}$$

$$\sigma_{23} = \lambda_{11}\lambda_{21}\phi_{12} \qquad \sigma_{24} = \lambda_{21}^2 \phi_{12} \qquad \sigma_{34} = \lambda_{11}\lambda_{21}\phi_{22}$$

$$[3.6]$$

To demonstrate identification, the parameters of the model must be solved for in terms of these equations.

Consider the parameters ϕ_{11} and ϕ_{22}. In solving for these parameters the variance equations σ_{11}, σ_{22}, σ_{33}, and σ_{44} are not helpful, since each contains an unknown parameter corresponding to the variance of a unique factor (parameters θ_{11}, θ_{22}, θ_{33}, and θ_{44}, respectively). Accordingly, the variance equations cannot be used to solve for ϕ_{11} and ϕ_{22} until the values of $\theta_{11}, \theta_{22}, \theta_{33}$, and θ_{44} are known. But solutions for $\theta_{11}, \theta_{22}, \theta_{33}$, and θ_{44} cannot be obtained until the parameters λ_{11}, λ_{21}, ϕ_{11}, and ϕ_{22} have been solved for. Consequently, if equation 3.6 can be solved for ϕ_{11} and ϕ_{22}, the equations for σ_{11}, σ_{22}, σ_{33}, and σ_{44} will not be helpful.

The equations for σ_{ij} ($i \neq j$) can be solved for ratios of ϕ_{11}, ϕ_{22}, and ϕ_{12}. The ratios $\phi_{11}/\phi_{12}, \phi_{11}/\phi_{22}$, and ϕ_{12}/ϕ_{22}, can be solved for in several ways; hence these *ratios* of parameters are overidentified. One set of solutions is

$$\frac{\sigma_{12}}{\sigma_{14}} = \frac{\phi_{11}}{\phi_{12}} \qquad \frac{\sigma_{12}}{\sigma_{34}} = \frac{\phi_{11}}{\phi_{22}} \qquad \frac{\sigma_{14}}{\sigma_{34}} = \frac{\phi_{12}}{\phi_{22}}$$

While there are three equations in three unknowns, they cannot be solved for the parameters ϕ_{11}, ϕ_{22}, and ϕ_{12}. (The reader is encouraged to try to solve these equations; such systems of equations are frequently encountered in attempts to identify a model.) Since the covariance equations cannot be solved for the parameters in Φ, these parameters are not identified.

A similar result occurs in attempting to solve for loadings λ_{11} and λ_{21}. While the ratio $\lambda_{11}/\lambda_{21}$ can be solved for in terms of covariances (e.g., $\lambda_{11}/\lambda_{21} = \sqrt{\sigma_{13}/\sigma_{24}}$), there are no solutions for λ_{11} and λ_{12} individually.

None of the parameters of model M_b are identified; hence the model is unidentified. The reason for this is that there is a *scale indeterminacy*, a basic problem in factor analytic models. //

Scale Indeterminacy and Setting a Metric

A factor analytic model cannot be identified until the metric, or scale, of the common factors has been established. If the scale of a factor is not established, there exists an indeterminacy between the variance of a common factor and the loadings of observed variables on that factor. This makes it impossible to distinguish between the case in which a factor has a large variance and the loadings on it are small, and the case in which the variance is small and the loadings on it are large. In terms of the parameters of the model, the problem is that if the loadings in Λ are not fixed, they must be estimated. If the diagonal elements of Φ (i.e., the variances of the common factors) are not fixed, they must be estimated. But it is not possible to estimate both the loadings on and the variances of common factors.

For example, let ξ be a common factor, let x be an observed variable that loads on ξ with loading λ, and let δ be the unique factor affecting x. For this example, subscripts have been dropped to simplify the presentation. The factor equation for x is

$$x = \lambda\xi + \delta \qquad [3.7]$$

Using the techniques and assumptions described above, it follows that

$$VAR(x) = \lambda^2 VAR(\xi) + VAR(\delta) \qquad [3.8]$$

To see why the loading of x on ξ and the variance of ξ are not identified, suppose that there is a second common factor, ξ^*, that differs from ξ only by a change in scale. That is, $\xi^* = \alpha\xi$, where α is any constant not equal to one or zero. For example, if ξ is measured in dollars and ξ^* is measured in cents, then α would equal 100 and ξ^* would equal $100 \times \xi$.

Now assume that the loading of x on ξ^* equals $\lambda^* = \lambda/\alpha$, resulting in the factor equation $x = \lambda^*\xi^* + \delta$. This equation is identical to equation 3.7, as can be easily shown:

$$x = \lambda^*\xi^* + \delta$$

$$= (\lambda/\alpha)(\alpha\xi) + \delta$$

$$= \lambda\xi + \delta \qquad [3.9]$$

Since $\xi^* = \alpha\xi$, it follows that $VAR(\xi^*) = VAR(\alpha\xi) = \alpha^2 VAR(\xi)$. This allows us to demonstrate that the variance of $x = \lambda^*\xi^* + \delta$ is equivalent to the variance of $x = \lambda\xi + \delta$ as defined in equation 3.8:

$$VAR(x) = \lambda^{*2} VAR(\xi^*) + VAR(\delta)$$

$$= (\lambda/\alpha)^2 VAR(\alpha\xi) + VAR(\delta)$$

$$= (\lambda^2/\alpha^2) \alpha^2 VAR(\xi) + VAR(\delta)$$

$$= \lambda^2 VAR(\xi) + VAR(\delta) \qquad [3.10]$$

Since the common and unique factors are unobserved, there is no way to tell if the observed variable x was generated by ξ and δ with a loading λ, or by ξ^* and δ with a loading λ^*. The change in scale occurring in the change from ξ to ξ^* is absorbed by an offsetting change in the loading from λ to $\lambda^* = \lambda/\alpha$. The loading of x on ξ and the variance of ξ cannot be identified since they are indistinguishable from the loading of x on ξ^* and the variance of ξ^*.

Example 1: scale indeterminacy. This important point can be further illustrated by considering the sets of specific values for Λ, Φ, and Θ presented above. Consider the observed variable x_3. The variance of x_3 was assumed to equal 1.60, or $\sigma_{33} = 1.60$. Set (1) of parameters included these values: $\lambda_{32}^{(1)} = 0.60$, $\phi_{22}^{(1)} = 3.0$, and $\theta_{33}^{(1)} = 0.52$. These values satisfy the covariance equation for x_3:

$$\sigma_{33} = \lambda_{32}^{(1)^2}\phi_{22}^{(1)} + \theta_{33}^{(1)}$$

or, substituting specific values,

$$1.60 = (0.60)^2\, 3.0 + 0.52$$

Now consider set (3) of parameters: $\lambda_{32}^{(3)} = 0.30$, $\phi_{22}^{(3)} = 12.00$, and $\theta_{33}^{(3)} = \theta_{33}^{(1)} = 0.52$. The loading λ_{32} decreases by a factor of 0.5 and the common factor variance ϕ_{22} increases by a factor of 4.0. Above it was demonstrated that if a common factor's scale is changed by a factor of α, the variance of the common factor changes by a factor of α^2, and the loadings on that factor change by a factor of $1/\alpha$. Thus, $\lambda_{32}^{(3)} = \lambda_{32}^{(1)}/\alpha$ and $\phi_{22}^{(3)} = \alpha^2\phi_{22}^{(1)}$, and α must equal 2.0. In moving from the parameters in set (1) to those in set (3), the decrease in the loading from 0.60 to 0.30 ($= 0.60 \times 1/2.0$) is offset by an increase in the variance of ξ_2 from 3.0 to 12.0 ($= 0.30 \times 2.0^2$). These results imply that

$$\sigma_{33} = \lambda_{32}^{(3)^2}\phi_{22}^{(3)} + \theta_{33}^{(3)} = (\lambda_{32}^{(1)}/\alpha)^2\alpha^2\phi_{22}^{(1)} + \theta_{33}^{(1)}$$

or, substituting specific values,

$$1.60 = (0.30)^2 12.0 + 0.52 = (0.60/2.0)^2[(2.0)^2 3.0] + 0.52$$

Thus, in terms of reproducing the variance of the observed variable x_3, the two sets of parameters are indistinguishable. The two solutions, as well as any other obtained by choosing a diagonal **M** matrix, differ only by the arbitrary scales of the common factors. The reader is encouraged to choose another diagonal **M** matrix and verify this statement. //

The indeterminacy caused by a lack of scale or metric for the common factors can be eliminated in either of two ways: (1) by fixing the variances of the common factors or (2) by fixing one loading on each factor to a nonzero value. To illustrate these two appraoches, consider again the factor equation $x = \lambda\xi + \delta$. Above it was noted that if the scale of the common factor is not known, it is impossible to distinguish the common factor ξ from the common factor $\xi^* = \alpha\xi$. If the variance of ξ is fixed to some constant value, say 1, then $VAR(\xi)$ and $VAR(\xi^*)$ must both equal one. Given the equality $VAR(\xi^*) = \alpha^2 VAR(\xi)$, it follows that α equals one and ξ is identical to ξ^*. Thus, the indeterminacy has been eliminated.

Alternatively, if the loading of the observed variable on the common factor is fixed to some constant value, say 1, the equality $\lambda\xi + \delta = \lambda^*\xi^* + \delta$ reduces to $\xi + \delta = \xi^* + \delta$ or $\xi = \xi^*$, and the indeterminacy has been eliminated. By fixing a loading to one, the common factor is given the scale of the observed variable. This can be seen by considering the factor equation $x = \lambda\xi + \delta$, which is now simplified by the assumption that $\lambda = 1.0$ to this: $x = \xi + \delta$. If ξ increases by some constant, an equivalent change is produced in the observed variable x. Since a common factor's scale is determined by a single fixed loading, it is unnecessary and overly restrictive to fix the loadings of more than one observed variable on any common factor.

In general, if the variances of the common factors are fixed or if one loading on each common factor is fixed, the scale indeterminacy is eliminated from the confirmatory factor model. This does not necessarily mean that the model is identified, for other sources of indeterminacy may still exist. These points are illustrated with Examples 1 and 2.

Example 1: identification. The first method of fixing the scale in the model is to constrain the diagonal elements of Φ to equal 1.0: $\phi_{11} = \phi_{22} = 1.0$. Let M_c be the model formed from M_a (see Table 3.1 for a summary of the models used in this example) by imposing the constraints $\phi_{11} = \phi_{22} = 1.0$. The resulting covariance equations are

$$\sigma_{11} = \lambda_{11}^2 + \theta_{11} \qquad\qquad \sigma_{22} = \lambda_{21}^2 + \theta_{22}$$

$$\sigma_{33} = \lambda_{32}^2 + \theta_{33} \qquad\qquad \sigma_{44} = \lambda_{42}^2 + \theta_{44}$$

$$\sigma_{12} = \lambda_{11}\lambda_{21} \qquad \sigma_{13} = \lambda_{11}\phi_{12}\lambda_{32} \qquad \sigma_{14} = \lambda_{11}\phi_{12}\lambda_{42}$$

$$\sigma_{23} = \lambda_{21}\phi_{12}\lambda_{32} \qquad \sigma_{24} = \lambda_{21}\phi_{12}\lambda_{42} \qquad \sigma_{34} = \lambda_{32}\lambda_{42}$$

From these equations we find that $\sigma_{12} = \lambda_{11}\lambda_{21}$ and $\sigma_{13}/\sigma_{23} = \lambda_{11}/\lambda_{21}$. Solving these two equations in two unknowns results in $\lambda_{21} = \sqrt{\sigma_{12}\sigma_{23}/\sigma_{13}}$ and $\lambda_{11} = \sigma_{12}/\lambda_{21}$. Similarly, $\lambda_{42} = \sqrt{\sigma_{34}\sigma_{14}/\sigma_{13}}$ and $\lambda_{32} = \sigma_{34}/\lambda_{42}$. Then, $\phi_{12} = \sigma_{13}/\lambda_{11}\lambda_{32}$. The remaining parameters are solved for as

$$\theta_{11} = \sigma_{11} - \lambda_{11}^2$$

$$\theta_{22} = \sigma_{22} - \lambda_{21}^2$$

$$\theta_{33} = \sigma_{33} - \lambda_{32}^2$$

$$\theta_{44} = \sigma_{44} - \lambda_{42}^2$$

Note that in proving that parameters are identified, once a parameter is shown to be identified, its value can be assumed known in proving that other parameters are identified. For example, once it was shown that λ_{21} was identified, λ_{21} was used to solve for λ_{11}.

Since each of the parameters is identified, the model is identified. Further, the model is overidentified. For example, parameter λ_{21} can also be solved for as $\lambda_{21} = \sqrt{\sigma_{12}\sigma_{24}/\sigma_{14}}$. Other parameters are also overidentified, as the reader should verify.

A second method of fixing the scales of the common factors is by fixing one of the loadings for each common factor to equal one. For example, constrain $\lambda_{11} = \lambda_{32} = 1.0$. Call this model M_d. The covariance equations are now

$\sigma_{11} = \phi_{11} + \theta_{11}$		$\sigma_{22} = \lambda_{21}^2\phi_{11} + \theta_{22}$
$\sigma_{33} = \phi_{22} + \theta_{33}$		$\sigma_{44} = \lambda_{42}^2\phi_{22} + \theta_{44}$
$\sigma_{12} = \lambda_{21}\phi_{11}$	$\sigma_{13} = \phi_{12}$	$\sigma_{14} = \lambda_{42}\phi_{12}$
$\sigma_{23} = \lambda_{21}\phi_{12}$	$\sigma_{24} = \lambda_{21}\phi_{12}\lambda_{42}$	$\sigma_{34} = \lambda_{42}\phi_{22}$

$$[3.11]$$

The parameters can be easily solved for as $\phi_{12} = \sigma_{13}$; $\lambda_{42} = \sigma_{14}/\phi_{12}$; $\lambda_{21} = \sigma_{23}/\phi_{12}$; $\phi_{11} = \sigma_{12}/\lambda_{21}$; $\phi_{22} = \sigma_{34}/\lambda_{42}$; $\theta_{11} = \sigma_{11} - \phi_{11}$; $\theta_{22} = \sigma_{22} - \lambda_{21}^2\phi_{11}$; $\theta_{33} = \sigma_{33} - \phi_{22}$; and $\theta_{44} = \sigma_{44} - \lambda_{42}^2\phi_{22}$. Hence, the model is identified.

Now consider a modification to Model M_b. The model, M_e, assumes that

$$\Lambda = \begin{bmatrix} \lambda_{11} & 0 \\ \lambda_{21} & 0 \\ 0 & \lambda_{11} \\ 0 & \lambda_{21} \end{bmatrix} \qquad \Phi = \begin{bmatrix} 1 & \phi_{12} \\ \phi_{21} & 1 \end{bmatrix}$$

and

$$\Theta = \begin{bmatrix} \theta_{11} & 0 & 0 & 0 \\ 0 & \theta_{22} & 0 & \theta_{24} \\ 0 & 0 & \theta_{33} & 0 \\ 0 & \theta_{42} & 0 & \theta_{44} \end{bmatrix}$$

The resulting covariance equations are

$$\sigma_{11} = \lambda_{11}^2 + \theta_{11} \qquad\qquad\qquad \sigma_{22} = \lambda_{21}^2 + \theta_{22}$$

$$\sigma_{33} = \lambda_{11}^2 + \theta_{33} \qquad\qquad\qquad \sigma_{44} = \lambda_{21}^2 + \theta_{44}$$

$$\sigma_{12} = \lambda_{11}\lambda_{21} \qquad \sigma_{13} = \lambda_{11}^2\phi_{12} \qquad \sigma_{14} = \lambda_{11}\phi_{12}\lambda_{21}$$

$$\sigma_{23} = \lambda_{21}\phi_{12}\lambda_{11} \qquad \sigma_{24} = \lambda_{21}^2\phi_{12} + \theta_{24} \qquad \sigma_{34} = \lambda_{11}\lambda_{21}$$

$$[3.12]$$

The parameters can be solved for as $\phi_{12} = \sigma_{23}/\sigma_{12}$; $\lambda_{11} = \sqrt{\sigma_{13}/\phi_{12}}$; $\lambda_{21} = \sigma_{34}/\lambda_{11}$; $\theta_{24} = \sigma_{24} - \lambda_{21}^2\phi_{12}$; and the θ_{ii} parameters are solved for similarly to the earlier models. Consequently, M_e is identified. Indeed, the model is overidentified, as the reader should attempt to verify.

As a final model, M_f in Table 3.1, modify M_e by relaxing the constraint $\theta_{13} = 0$. The only equation that changes in equation set 3.12 is $\sigma_{13} = \lambda_{11}^2\phi_{12} + \theta_{13}$. The covariance between ξ_1 and ξ_2 (which is now a correlation since ξ_1 and ξ_2 have variances of one), can still be solved, and is in fact overidentified: $\phi_{12} = \sigma_{23}/\sigma_{34} = \sigma_{14}/\sigma_{34} = \sigma_{14}/\sigma_{12} = \sigma_{23}/\sigma_{12}$. The covariance equations cannot be solved for any other parameters; therefore the model is unidentified. It is important to realize that even though the model is not identified, it would be possible to estimate ϕ_{12}, since it is identified. If a researcher were primarily concerned with the correlation between the two common factors, it could be estimated, even though the other parameters could not. //

Example 2: identification. The easiest way to prove identification of the MMMT model is to use Jöreskog's sufficient condition. Four requirements must be satisfied:

(1) Φ must be a symmetric, positive definite matrix with diagonal elements equal to 1.0. As the model was first presented, the diagonal elements of Φ were not constrained to equal 1.0. However, it is necessary to set the scale of the factors in the MMMT model, just as in our last example. If this is done by fixing the variances of the common factors to equal 1.0, the first condition is satisfied.

(2) Θ is diagonal. This was assumed in our initial specification.

(3) Λ has at least $(s - 1) = 5$ fixed zeros in each column, where s is the number of latent variables. This is easily verified by inspecting the Λ matrix presented earlier.

(4) Λ^k has rank $(s - 1) = 5$, where Λ^k (for k = 1,6) is the submatrix of Λ consisting of the rows of Λ that have fixed zero elements in the kth column. This can be readily verified by constructing the required submatrices.

Thus, each condition is satisfied and the model is identified. //

This concludes our discussion of identification. While the algebraic manipulations may seem far removed from the substantive interest motivating a particular analysis, identification is a crucial component of the confirmatory factor model.

4. ESTIMATION OF THE CONFIRMATORY FACTOR MODEL

After identification has been established, estimation can proceed. The general objective in estimating the factor model is to find estimates of the parameters that reproduce the sample matrix of variances and covariances of the observed variables as closely as possible in some well-defined sense. In this chapter several methods of estimation are presented. While a formal statistical justification of these methods is beyond the scope of this monograph, it is possible to present the general characteristics of each method. For technical details, see Browne, (1974), Jöreskog and Goldberger (1972), Bentler and Bonett (1980), and the literature cited therein.

The researcher begins with a sample of observed data. From the sample data it is possible to construct the sample covariance matrix S with elements s_{ij}. Diagonal elements are variances of the observed variables, and off-diagonal elements are covariances. If the data are standardized, S contains the correlations among the observed variables.

The population covariance matrix Σ is related to the population parameters by the covariance equation $\Sigma = \Lambda \Phi \Lambda' + \Theta$. In the same way an estimate of Σ is defined in terms of estimates of the population parameters through the covariance equation $\hat{\Sigma} = \hat{\Lambda} \hat{\Phi} \hat{\Lambda}' + \hat{\Theta}$, where the $\wedge$ indicates that the matrices contain estimates of population parameters. These estimates must satisfy the constraints that have been imposed on the model. Estimation involves finding values of $\hat{\Lambda}$, $\hat{\Phi}$, and $\hat{\Theta}$ that generate an estimated covariance matrix $\hat{\Sigma}$ that is as close as possible to the sample covariance matrix S.

It is useful to think of the process of estimation as follows. Consider all possible sets of matrices having the dimensions of the matrices Λ, Φ, and Θ. Many of these possible matrices must be excluded from consideration because they do not incorporate the constraints imposed on Λ, Φ, and Θ. Let Λ^*, Φ^*, and Θ^* be any matrices that incorporate the imposed constraints. This set of matrices define a matrix Σ^* according to the formula $\Sigma^* = \Lambda^* \Phi^* \Lambda^{*'} + \Theta^*$. If Σ^* is "close" to S, one might conclude that Λ^*, Φ^*, and Θ^* are reasonable estimates of the population parameters. This would be justified since the value of Σ^* implied by Λ^*, Φ^*, and Θ^* is consistent with the observed data. The problems of estimation are to measure how close Σ^* is to S, and to find the values of Λ^*, Φ^*, and Θ^* that produce the Σ^* that is as close as possible to S.

A function that measures how close a given Σ^* is to the sample covariance matrix S is called a *fitting function*. A fitting function is designated as $F(S;\Sigma^*)$; or, to indicate that Σ^* is defined by Λ^*, Φ^*, and Θ^*, it may be written as $F(S;\Lambda^*, \Phi^*, \Theta^*)$. This function is defined over all possible matrices Λ^*, Φ^*, and Θ^* that satisfy the constraints on Λ, Φ, and Θ. If one set of "*"ed matrices produces the matrix Σ_1^*, and a second set produces the matrix Σ_2^*, if $F(S;\Sigma_1^*) < F(S; \Sigma_2^*)$, Σ_1^* is considered to be closer to S than is Σ_2^*. Those values of Λ^*, Φ^*, and Θ^*

that minimize the fitting function for a given **S** are the sample estimates of the population parameters and are designated as $\hat{\Lambda}$, $\hat{\Phi}$, and $\hat{\Theta}$.

Three fitting functions are commonly used in confirmatory factor analysis. These functions correspond to the methods of unweighted least squares (ULS), generalized least squares (GLS), and maximum likelihood (ML).

Unweighted Least Squares

ULS for the confirmatory factor model corresponds to the method of iterated principal factors or MINRES in exploratory factor analysis (see Harmon, 1976: chaps.8, 9). The ULS estimators of Λ, Φ, and Θ are those values that minimize the fitting function:

$$F_{ULS}(S;\Sigma^*) = tr[(S - \Sigma^*)^2] \qquad [4.1]$$

where "tr" is the trace operator indicating the sum of the diagonal elements of a matrix. [14] The fitting function for ULS is an intuitively reasonable way of assessing the difference between two matrices. Though not immediately obvious from equation 4.1, the fitting function computes the sum of the squares of corresponding elements of **S** and Σ^*. Estimation involves minimizing this sum of squares, in much the same way that ordinary or unweighted least squares for regression analysis minimizes the sum of the squared residuals.

Beyond this intuitive justification, the ULS estimator can be shown to be consistent without making any assumptions about the distribution of the x-variables (Bentler and Weeks, 1980). This means that for large samples, ULS is approximately unbiased. Not having to make distributional assumptions about the observed variables is an advantage, but it is offset by two limitations. First, there are no statistical tests associated with ULS estimation of the confirmatory factor model. Second, ULS estimators have a property known as *scale dependency*.

Scale Dependency

The scale of a variable changes if the unit of measurement changes. Accompanying a change in scale of a variable is a corresponding change in the standard deviation of that variable. For example, if income is measured in cents rather than dollars, the change in scale is accompanied by an increase by a factor of 100 (the number of cents in a dollar) in the standard deviation. A particularly useful change in scale involves standardization. If a variable is divided by its standard deviation, the resulting variable has a standard deviation of one and the covariance between two such standardized variables is the correlation between those variables.

A method of estimation is scale free if the minimum of the fitting function is independent of the scale of the variables. Accordingly, the minimum of the fitting function for a scale free estimator is identical, whether the sample covariance matrix or the sample correlation matrix is analyzed. The parameter estimates would change, but only to reflect the change in scale of the observed variables being analyzed. An example clarifies this point.

Let x be an observed variable that measures income in dollars, and let ξ be a common factor measuring income. Let $\lambda = 5$ be the loading of x on ξ, indicating that a unit change in ξ results in a five-dollar change in x. If the scale of x is changed from dollars to cents, a change by a factor of 100, the value of λ changes to 500 to reflect the change in scale. Thus, a change in ξ of one unit would result in a change in the rescaled x of 500 cents, the new unit of measurement. (Recall that we are assuming the estimates are obtained by a scale-free method of estimation.) Clearly this is a transparent change, since 500 units in the rescaled x is equal to five units in the original x. That is, 500 cents is equal to five dollars.

If a method is scale dependent, changes in scale result in different minimums for the fitting function, and changes in the estimates do not simply reflect the change in scale. ULS is a method of estimation that is scale dependent. Accordingly, the results obtained may differ when different units of measurement are used. For example, analyzing data in which income is measured in dollars can lead to substantively different results than those obtained from analyzing the same data measured in cents, pounds, or yen. Since the scales of variables are often arbitrary, it is generally suggested that when a scale-dependent method is used, the scales of the observed variables should be standardized by analyzing a correlation matrix.

Generalized Least Squares and Maximum Likelihood

GLS and ML are two methods that have the advantage of being scale free. These methods are now considered.

The fitting function for GLS is more complex than that for ULS, with differences between S and Σ being weighted by elements of S^{-1} (see Jöreskog and Goldberger, 1972). The GLS fitting function is [15]

$$F_{GLS}(S;\Sigma^*) = tr[(S - \Sigma^*)S^{-1}]^2 \qquad [4.2]$$

As Σ^* approaches S, the value of F_{GLS} becomes smaller. If S equals Σ^*, the function necessarily equals zero.

The ML estimator minimizes the fitting function defined as

$$F_{ML}(S;\Sigma^*) = tr(S\Sigma^{*-1}) + [\log | \Sigma^*| - \log | S |] - q \qquad [4.3]$$

where $\log | \Sigma^* |$ is the log of the determinant of the matrix Σ^*.[16,17] The statistical justification of this function is beyond the scope of this discussion, but it is possible to indicate how the function reflects the distance between S and Σ^*. (See Jöreskog [1969] for a derivation of the ML fitting function.) If S and Σ^* are similar, their inverses will be similar. Accordingly, $S\Sigma^{*-1}$ becomes closer to a $(q \times q)$ identity matrix as Σ^* and S become closer. Since the trace of a $(q \times q)$ identity matrix equals q (the sum of the q ones on the diagonal), the first term in the fitting function approaches the value of q as S and Σ^* become closer. The second term in F_{ML} is the difference in the logs of the determinants of S and Σ^*. As S and Σ^* become closer, their determinants (and logs of determinants) become closer and the second term approaches zero. The last term in the fitting function is the constant q, which serves to cancel the value approached by the first term. Accordingly, if S and Σ^* are equal, the fitting function will equal zero.

If x has a multivariate normal distribution, both GLS and ML have desirable asymptotic properties, that is, properties that hold as the sample size gets large. The ML estimator is approximately unbiased, has as small a sampling variance as any other estimator, and is approximately normally distributed. This means that if the assumptions about the distribution of x hold, as the sample size gets larger, (1) the expected value of the sample estimates get closer and closer to the true population parameters; (2) the variance of the sampling distribution of the ML estimators becomes as small as possible with any estimator; and (3) the sampling distribution of the estimators becomes normal. In the confirmatory factor model, GLS is asymptotically equivalent to ML (Lee, 1977; Browne, 1974). Both methods of estimation are scale invariant and have desirable properties for statistical testing, a topic discussed in the next chapter.

Note that these are asymptotic properties. Strictly speaking, they are justified only as the sample approaches an infinite size. An important practical question is, How large must a sample be in order to take advantage of the desirable asymptotic properties? Unfortunately, there is no definitive answer to this question. Boomsma (1982) has obtained some results for two factor models with either six or eight observed variables. For such models he concluded that it is dangerous to use sample sizes smaller than 100. One would expect that more complex models with more factors and more observed variables would require larger samples. Further, he found that the robustness of the ML estimator depends on the magnitudes of the parameters being estimated. Further research is needed in this area.

The mathematical justification for both GLS and ML require assumptions of normality, with GLS being justified under slightly less restrictive assumptions than ML (Browne, 1974). Unfortunately, very little is known about the effects of violations of the assumption of normality on the properties of either GLS or ML estimators for the confirmatory factor model.

Practical Considerations

In general, none of these estimators (ULS, GLS, and ML) have closed-form solutions.[18] That is to say, the values that minimize the fitting functions must be found by numerically searching over possible values of Λ, Φ, and Θ. The estimates are those values that make the fitting function as small as possible. Technical details on how the search is conducted need not concern us, even though without computer programs implementing efficient search procedures the application of the confirmatory factor model would not be possible. Three practical problems are, however, worth noting.

First, it is possible for search procedures to locate what is called a "local minimum." This is a value of the fitting function that appears to be the smallest possible when actually there are other smaller values. Such occurrences are thought to be rare, but are nonetheless possible (see Jöreskog and Sörbom, 1981: I.31).

Second, the values of the parameters that minimize the fitting function may be outside the range of feasible values. For example, a variance may be estimated to be negative or a correlation to be greater than 1.0. Such occurrences are thought to result from misspecified models or insufficiently large sample sizes. This issue is discussed in more detail in the next chapter.

Third, numerical searches can be costly in computer time. The computer time required for estimating a given model is based on several things: (1) The larger the number of independent elements in the covariance matrix for the observed variables, the more costly it is to estimate a given model. Note that the number of elements in S goes up according to the formula $q(q + 1)/2$, which increases much more quickly than the number of observed variables, q. (2) The more parameters to be estimated, the more computer time required. (3) The better the guess of the values of the parameters to estimated, the less computer time required. Software estimating the confirmatory factor model requires start values for each parameter that is to be estimated. Start values are guesses that the user supplies, which are used to compute the first Σ^*. The software proceeds by refining these initial guesses. The closer the start values, the easier it will be to find the final estimates. Unfortunately, choosing start values can be difficult. If there are similar models using similar data that have been analyzed by others, these can provide suggestions of start values. Alternatively, the user must guess start values on the basis of knowledge of the process being modeled. On the brighter side, the most recent version of LISREL (Jöreskog and Sörbom, 1981) has incorporated an algorithm for generating start values for most models. This can save the user a great deal of time and substantially reduce the cost of estimating models.

In this discussion of the cost of estimating a model, there has been a conspicuous lack of concern for sample size. This is because once the covariance matrix for the observed variables has been computed (an operation whose cost does depend on sample size), the cost of estimating a confirmatory factor model is independent of sample size. This can be seen by noting that none of the fitting functions includes a term reflecting the number of observations in the sample.

5. ASSESSMENT OF FIT IN THE CONFIRMATORY FACTOR MODEL

Estimating the parameters of a confirmatory factor model is only the first step. In a confirmatory analysis there are specific hypotheses to test; in an exploratory analysis some indication of how to improve the fit of the model is desired. A variety of techniques are available for these purposes. The values of individual parameter estimates and their standard errors can be used to test the statistical significance of individual parameters. A chi-square goodness-of-fit test can be used to assess the overall fit of a model and to compare competing, nested models (defined below). Indices based on derivatives of the fitting function can be used to suggest better-fitting models. The following discussion of these techniques draws heavily upon Jöreskog and Sörbom (1981) and Bentler and Bonnet (1980).

Examining Values of the Parameters

In most programs that estimate the confirmatory factor model no constraints are imposed to ensure that the estimates have meaningful values. Consequently, it is possible to obtain negative estimates of variances and / or correlations that exceed 1.0 in absolute value. Even if all other measures of goodness of fit suggest that the model is adequate, unreasonable estimates indicate that one of the following problems has occurred (Jöreskog and Sörbom, 1981: I.36).

First, the model may be misspecified. This can be the case even when the overall fit of the model is adequate.

Second, there may be violations of the assumed normality of the observed variables. Very little is known about the robustness of ML and GLS estimation of the confirmatory factor model when the assumption of normality has been violated. Since estimation by ULS does not require assumptions of normality, violations of normality cannot be the cause of unreasonable ULS estimates.

Third, the sample may be too small to justify the use of the asymptotic properties of the method of estimation. Boomsma (1982) found that small samples often result in negative estimates of variances.

Fourth, the model may be nearly unidentified, making the estimation of some parameters difficult and unstable. This problem is sometimes referred to as empirical underidentification (Kenny, 1979: 40, 143, 155). It occurs when the model can be proven identified, but the sample data are such that the method of estimation has a difficult time distinguishing between two or more of the parameters. This issue is discussed further in the next section in relation to the correlations among estimates.

Fifth, the covariance matrix may have been computed by pairwise deletion of missing data. When missing data is a problem, researchers often construct covariance or correlation matrices by using all of the data available for a given pair of variables to compute the covariance or correlation between those two variables (see Hertel, 1976). As a result, each covariance or correlation is based on a different sample. This can lead to a covariance matrix that is inappropriate to use for estimation. In extreme cases programs for ML or GLS estimation may detect the inappropriate matrix and refuse to analyze it; in less extreme cases the matrix may be analyzed, but may result in erroneous estimates. ULS estimation generally proceeds, regardless of the inputted covariance matrix. A pairwise covariance matrix should be used only if there are a small number of missing observations scattered evenly across the variables and cases.

Variances and Covariances of the Estimates

Using the assumptions justifying either ML or GLS estimation, it is possible to estimate the variances of individual parameter estimates, which can be used to test hypotheses about individual parameters. Let ω be any parameter to be estimated from the model; let $\hat{\omega}$ be an estimate of ω; and let $\hat{\sigma}$ be the estimate of the standard deviation of the sampling distribution of $\hat{\omega}$. Under the assumptions justifying ML or GLS estimation, for large samples $\hat{\omega}$ is distributed approximately normally with a standard deviation estimated as $\hat{\sigma}$. This result allows us to test hypotheses of the sort, H_0: $\omega = \omega^*$, where ω^* is a fixed value (generally zero). To test this hypothesis the test statistic $z = (\hat{\omega} - \omega^*)/\hat{\sigma}$ can be used. For large samples z is approximately normally distributed with a mean of zero and a variance of one.[19] For example, if $\hat{\phi}_{12} = 0.78$ and $\hat{\sigma}_{\phi_{12}} = 0.56$, then $z - (0.78 - 0.00)/0.56 = 1.39$, and the null hypothesis (H_0: $\phi_{12} = 0$) would not be rejected at the .05 level. The researcher would conclude that ϕ_{12} is not significantly different from zero.

Under the assumptions of ML and GLS, covariances among estimates can also be estimated. Let ω_1 and ω_2 be any two parameters, estimated as $\hat{\omega}_1$ and $\hat{\omega}_2$. Let their standard deviations be estimated as $\hat{\sigma}_1$ and $\hat{\sigma}_2$, and their covariance estimated as $\hat{\sigma}_{12}$. The correlation between the estimates of ω_1 and ω_2 can be computed as $\hat{\rho}_{12} = \hat{\sigma}_{12}/\hat{\sigma}_1\hat{\sigma}_2$. If $\hat{\rho}_{12}$ is large, this indicates that changes in the estimate of ω_1 are associated with corresponding changes in the estimate of ω_2. Accordingly, it is statistically difficult to disentangle these two parameters, even though both are identified. This is the problem of empirical underidentification that was discussed earlier. Readers familiar with multiple regression should recognize this as being comparable to the effects of extreme multicollinearity (Jöreskog and Sörbom, 1981: I.36: Judge et al., 1980: chap. 12).

Chi-Square Goodness-of-Fit Tests

Under the assumptions justifying ML and GLS, a chi-square goodness-of-fit measure can be computed. (See Bentler and Weeks [1980] for a statistical justification of this test.) This statistic allows a test of the null hypothesis H_0 that a given model provides an acceptable fit of the observed data. The fit of the model is assessed by comparing the observed covariance matrix S with the covariance matrix estimated by the equation $\hat{\Sigma} = \hat{\Lambda}\hat{\Phi}\hat{\Lambda}' + \hat{\Theta}$. $\hat{\Sigma}$ will not perfectly reproduce S, since the values that $\hat{\Sigma}$ can assume are limited by the constraints imposed on the model's parameters. The chi-square goodness-of-fit test compares the imperfect fit under H_0 to the perfect fit under the alternative hypothesis H_1 that Σ is any covariance matrix. The larger the differences between S and $\hat{\Sigma}$, the larger the chi-square.

As with any chi-square statistic, there are degrees of freedom associated with the test. In the confirmatory factor model the degrees of freedom are computed as

$$df = \text{number of independent parameters under } H_1 \text{ minus}$$
$$\text{number of independent parameters under } H_0 \qquad [5.1]$$

The number of independent parameters under H_1 is easily computed. Since H_1 provides a perfect fit of the data, there must be one independent parameter for each independent element of Σ—specifically, $q(q + 1)/2$ independent parameters, where q is the number of observed variables. The number of independent parameters associated with H_0 varies with each model. The only difficulty in counting the parameters involves determining which are independent. Since covariance matrices are symmetric, if parameters above the diagonal are counted, those below the diagonal must not be counted. For example, since $\phi_{12} = \phi_{21}$, if ϕ_{12} is counted as an independent parameter, then ϕ_{21} cannot be counted. Further, equality constraints must be taken into account. If several parameters are constrained to be equal, only one of those parameters is independent. For example, if the model assumes that $\lambda_{11} = \lambda_{12} = \lambda_{13}$, then only one of the three λ parameters can be counted as independent. Examples of counting degrees of freedom are given below.

Testing proceeds by finding the critical value at the α level of significance of the chi-square distribution with df degrees of freedom. Call this value $\chi_{1-\alpha}(df)$. Values of the chi-square larger than the critical value result in the rejection of the null hypothesis and the conclusion that the proposed model did not generate the observed data; values smaller than the critical value result in the acceptance of the null hypothesis and the conclusion that the proposed model did generate the observed data.

While the chi-square test can be derived theoretically under the assumptions necessary for ML or GLS estimation, Bentler and Bonett (1980) and Jöreskog and Sörbom (1981: I.38) noted that applications of the chi-square test are often unjustified in practice. To apply the test it must be assumed that (1) the observed variables are normally distributed, (2) the analysis is based on a sample covariance matrix rather than a sample correlation matrix, and (3) the sample size is large enough to justify the asymptotic properties of the chi-square test. At least one of these assumptions is generally violated in applications of the confirmatory factor model. Consequently, Jöreskog and Sörbom suggested that the chi-square test be used as an indicator of how well the model reproduces the observed covariance matrix S, rather than as a formal test of a hypothesis. A large value of the chi-square indicates a poor reproduction of S, and a small value indicates a good reproduction.

Nested Models and Difference of Chi-Square Tests

In many cases it is useful to compare the hyothesis implied by a given model to the hypothesis implied by some competing model. Such tests are possible when the two models are *nested*.

For any two models (call them M_1 and M_2) M_1 is nested in M_2 if M_1 can be obtained from M_2 by constraining one or more of the free parameters in M_2 to be fixed or equal to other parameters. Thus, M_1 can be thought of as a special case of M_2. Two examples illustrate this concept.

Example 1: nested models. Consider the models M_d, M_g, and M_h for the measurement of psychological disorders:

Model	λ_{11}	λ_{21}	λ_{32}	λ_{42}	ϕ_{11}	ϕ_{22}	ϕ_{12}	θ_{11}	θ_{22}	θ_{33}	θ_{44}	θ_{24}
M_d	1	*	1	*	*	*	*	*	*	*	*	0
M_g	1	A	1	A	B	B	*	*	*	*	*	0
M_h	1	A	1	A	B	B	*	*	*	*	*	*

An * indicates that the parameter is free; numbers indicate the value that a parameter has been constrained to equal; and letters indicate pairs of parameters that are constrained to be equal.

M_g can be formed from M_d by imposing the constraints $\lambda_{21} = \lambda_{42}$ and $\phi_{11} = \phi_{22}$. Accordingly, M_g is nested in M_d. Similarly, M_g is nested in M_h, since M_g can be formed from M_h by constraining θ_{24} to equal zero. M_d is not nested in M_h, nor is M_h nested in M_d, since neither model can be formed by imposing constraints on the other model. //

Example 2: nested models. As originally specified, our multimethod-multitrait model assumed that all trait and method factors were correlated. Except for ones on the diagonal, Φ was unconstrained. Call this version of the MMMT model M_A. In some applications it is reasonable to assume that trait factors are independent of method factors. For our example this implies that

$$
\Phi = \begin{bmatrix}
\underline{1.0} & \phi_{12} & \phi_{13} & \underline{0.0} & \underline{0.0} & \underline{0.0} \\
\phi_{21} & \underline{1.0} & \phi_{23} & \underline{0.0} & \underline{0.0} & \underline{0.0} \\
\phi_{31} & \phi_{32} & \underline{1.0} & \underline{0.0} & \underline{0.0} & \underline{0.0} \\
\underline{0.0} & \underline{0.0} & \underline{0.0} & \underline{1.0} & \phi_{45} & \phi_{46} \\
\underline{0.0} & \underline{0.0} & \underline{0.0} & \phi_{54} & \underline{1.0} & \phi_{56} \\
\underline{0.0} & \underline{0.0} & \underline{0.0} & \phi_{64} & \phi_{65} & \underline{1.0}
\end{bmatrix}
= \begin{bmatrix}
\text{trait/} & \text{trait/} \\
\text{trait} & \text{method} \\
\hline
\text{method/} & \text{method/} \\
\text{trait} & \text{method}
\end{bmatrix}
$$

Call this version of the MMMT model M_B. A third version of the model—call it M_C—assumes that all factors are uncorrelated. That is, that $\Phi = I$, an identity matrix.

M_B can be formed from M_A by constraining correlations in the method/trait and trait/method blocks of Φ to equal zero. Hence, M_B is nested in M_A. M_C can be formed from M_A by constraining all off-diagonal elements of Φ to zero; accordingly, it is also nested in M_A. Finally, M_C is nested in M_B, since it can be formed from M_B by constraining the remaining off-diagonal elements of Φ to zero.

The reader should realize that for models M_B and M_C to be estimated, they must be identified, which in fact they are. For details on these models, see Alwin (1974). //

Nested models can be statistically compared. If M_1 is nested in M_2, a difference of chi-square test can be used to compare M_1 with the more general model M_2. The more general model M_2 necessarily fits as well as or better than M_1, since it has at least one additional unconstrained parameter to aid in reproducing the observed covariance matrix. The estimated covariance matrix Σ_2 obtained from estimating M_2 will be closer to S than Σ_1 obtained from estimating M_1. As a consequence, the X_1^2 with df_1 degrees of freedom from testing M_1 will necessarily be larger than the X_2^2 with df_2 degrees of freedom obtained from testing M_2. Whether this improvement in fit obtained by adding additional parameters to M_1 is statistically significant is determined by a difference of chi-square test. For large samples, $X^2 = X_1^2 - X_2^2$ is distributed as chi-square with df $= df_1 - df_2$ degrees of freedom if M_1 is the true model. If X^2 exceeds the chosen critical value for the chi-square distribution with df degrees of freedom, the hypothesis that the constraints imposed on M_2 to form M_1 are valid can be rejected. That is, relaxing the constraints results in a statistically significant improvement in fit of M_2 over M_1.

Example 1: difference of chi-square test. Consider models M_g with a chi-square of X_g^2 and $df_g = 3$ degrees of freedom, and M_h with X_h^2 and $df_h = 2$. Model M_g differs from M_h in that the parameter θ_{24} is constrained to equal zero in M_g. To test the hypothesis H_0: $\theta_{24} = 0$ in M_h, the difference of chi-square test $X^2 = X_g^2 - X_h^2$ with df $= df_g - df_h = 1$ can be used. If X^2 exceeds the critical value of the chi-square distribution with one degree of freedom at a given level of significance, the null hypothesis that $\theta_{24} = 0$ would be rejected. Note that H_0 could also be tested with the z-test described above.

The difference of chi-square test is particularly useful in testing more complex hypotheses. Consider models M_g with X_g^2 and $df_g = 3$, and M_d with X_d^2 and $df_d = 1$. Model M_g differs from M_d in that the loading of x_2 on ξ_1 is constrained to equal the loading of x_4 on ξ_2 (i.e., $\lambda_{21} = \lambda_{42}$) in M_g, and the variance of ξ_1 is constrained to equal the variance of ξ_2 (i.e., $\phi_{11} = \phi_{22}$) in M_g. To test the hypothesis H_0: $\lambda_{21} = \lambda_{42}$ and $\phi_{11} = \phi_{22}$ in M_g, the difference of chi-square test $X^2 = X_g^2 - X_d^2$ with df $= df_g - df_d = 2$ can be used. If X^2 exceeds the critical value of the chi-square distribu-tion with df degrees of freedom at a given level of significance, the null hypothesis would be rejected. Note that this complex hypothesis could not be tested with a simple z-test. //

Example 2: difference of chi-square test. For the MMMT model, let X_A^2, X_B^2, and X_C^2 be the chi-square test associated with models M_A, M_B, and M_C with df_A, df_B, and df_C degrees of freedom. Recall that in M_A, Φ is unconstrained except for ones on the diagonal; in M_B the method/trait blocks of Φ are constrained to zeros; and in M_C, Φ is constrained to equal I. The hypothesis that all factors are uncorrelated can be tested by comparing M_A with M_C. The resulting test statistic is: $X^2 = X_C^2 - X_A^2$ with df $= df_C - df_A$. If X^2 exceeded the appropriate critical value, the hypothesis that the factors were uncorrelated would be rejected. The hypothesis that the method/trait correlations are zero, but the method/method and trait/trait correlations are not zero can be tested by comparing models M_A and M_B. The appropriate test statistic is $X^2 = X_B^2 - X_A^2$ with $df_B - df_A$ degrees of freedom. //

Specification Searches

If the hypothesized model does not fit, it is often of interest to find a model that does fit. Given that the model suggested by theory has already been rejected, there may be little theoretical guidance as to how to improve the fit of the model. Consequently, the results obtained from estimating the rejected model will have to be used to suggest additional, perhaps better-fitting, models. This process is called a specification search.

While a specification search can provide useful information, it is important to realize that since the sample data are used to select a model, the same data cannot be used to formally assess the fit of that model (Leamer, 1978). The model selected must be viewed as tentative, in need of verification with a second, independent sample. With this important warning in mind, procedures for searching for a model are considered.

The first and most obvious way to improve the fit of a model is to eliminate parameters that are not significant, as indicated by a z-test. Restricting such parameters cannot reduce the magnitude of a chi-square obtained, but can improve the overall fit by recovering degrees of freedom with little accompanying increase in the chi-square. For example, assume that a model—call it M_1—with five degrees of freedom was fit with a resulting chi-square of 10.4. Since the critical value at the .10 level of significance is 9.24, M_1 would be rejected. Now suppose that M_1 had five parameters with very small z-values, indicating that they were not significantly different from zero. By constraining these parameters to zero a second model, M_2, is formed with 10 degrees of freedom. The .10 critical value for the chi-square test is increased to 15.99 as a result of the added degrees of freedom. The chi-square obtained in testing M_2 also increases, since M_2 has fewer parameters with which to reproduce the observed covariance matrix. Nevertheless, if the resulting chi-square is still less than 15.99, M_2 would be considered an acceptably fitting model. The increase in the chi-square would have been offset by the accompanying increase in degrees of freedom.

The ability of a model to reproduce the observed covariance matrix can also be improved by the addition of parameters. To determine which parameters might improve the fit of a model, it is sometimes proposed that the matrix of differences between the observed covariance matrix S and the predicted matrix $\hat{\Sigma}$ be studied. The argument is that large differences reflect the portion of the model that is misspecified. This notion is misleading, however, since the methods of estimation used for the confirmatory factor model are full-information techniques. A full-information technique *simultaneously* fits all of the parameters in all of the equations of the model. Specification errors in one equation affect the estimation of other, correctly specified equations. Accordingly, modifying a model on the basis of the differences in $S - \hat{\Sigma}$ does not necessarily result in an improvement in fit (Sörbom, 1975).

A more promising approach is based on the partial derivatives of the fitting function with respect to each of the fixed parameters of the model (Sörbom, 1975). The partial derivatives indicate the rate of change in the fitting function for a very small change in a fixed parameter. Thus, if a derivative with respect to a particular fixed parameter is large, relaxing that parameter might lead to a large decrease in the minimum of the fitting function, hence, a substantial improvement in the fit of the model. Unfortunately, this is not always the case. A fixed parameter that has a large derivative may have a fixed value very close to the value that would be estimated if that parameter were freed. If this were the case, the improvement in fit would be small.

To remedy this problem, Jöreskog and Sörbom (1981: I.42) have proposed a *modification index* that is equal to the expected decrease in the chi-square if a single constraint is relaxed. The actual decrease in the chi-square may be larger than the expected value, but it should not be smaller. The greatest improvement in fit for a given model is obtained by freeing the parameter with the largest modification index. Since freeing a single parameter results in a loss of one degree of freedom, the modification index approximates a chi-square test of the hypothesis that the parameter to be freed is equal to its fixed value. If the value of the modification index for a parameter does not exceed 3.84—the 0.05 critical value for a chi-square test with one degree of freedom—no appreciable gain in fit is likely to result from freeing that parameter.

In using the modification index (or the derivative), it is suggested that only one parameter be relaxed at a time, since freeing one parameter may reduce or eliminate the improvement in fit possible by freeing a second parameter. The parameter to be relaxed should have the largest modification index *and* it must make substantive sense to relax that parameter.[20] This procedure continues, relaxing one parameter at a time, until an adequate fit is found or no further improvement in fit is possible. This is a blatantly exploratory approach. The resulting model should be verified with a second, independent sample. Further, there is no guarantee that the models suggested by the modification indices are identified. The user must prove identification for each model estimated in a specification search.

This concludes our survey of the basic techniques for assessing goodness of fit and carrying out specification searches in the confirmatory factor model. Additional techniques and greater detail can be found in Jöreskog and Sörbom (1981) and Bentler and Bonett (1980). This chapter concludes with an extended example and a discussion of standardized solutions.

Example 1: estimation and hypothesis testing. The model for the measurement of psychological disorders, though quite simple, can be used to illustrate a number of basic ideas. First, results of the three methods of estimation are compared.[21] Second, various ways of establishing the metric of the latent variables are demonstrated. Third, a specification search is performed. And finally, the idea of scale invariance is extended to deal with models containing equality constraints.

The first model considered, M_d, corresponds to the solid lines in Figure 5.1. The metric is set by constraining the loadings for x_1 and x_3 to equal 1.0 ($\lambda_{11} = \lambda_{32} = 1$). Table 5.1 presents the ULS, GLS, and ML estimates for this model. The GLS and ML estimates are extremely close, while the ULS estimates are slightly different. This pattern of similarities is found in a variety of models using various data sets. The best way to assess the similarity of the results is to determine if the substantive interpretations that each set of estimates generate are similar. In a factor model of this sort there are two functions of parameters that are of primary interest: correlations between common factors and reliabilities of observed variables.

Estimates of correlations among the latent variables differ from the correlations among the observed variables, since the latter correlations are affected by errors in measurement. To estimate the correlation between ξ_1 and ξ_2, the general formula for the correlation coefficient can be used:

$$COR(\xi_1,\xi_2) = COV(\xi_1, \xi_2) \,/\, \sqrt{VAR(\xi_1)\ VAR(\xi_2)}$$

$$= \phi_{12} \,/\, \sqrt{\phi_{11}\phi_{22}}$$

The correlations between the latent variables in M_d range from 0.63 to 0.66 (see Table 5.1), indicating that the latent variables for psychological disorders at time 1 and time 2 share between 40% (= 0.63^2) and 44% (= 0.66^2) of their variation in common. The correlations between the observed variables are uniformly smaller. The correlation between the number of psychological symptoms at the two times is 0.53, and the

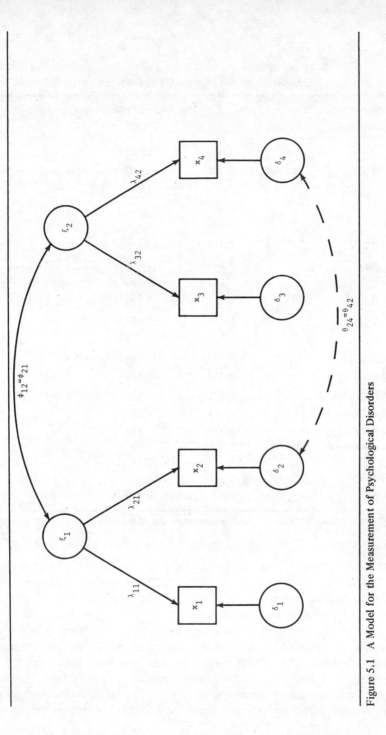

Figure 5.1 A Model for the Measurement of Psychological Disorders

71

TABLE 5.1
Estimation Model M_d, by ULS, GLS, and ML

Parameter	Method of Estimation		
	ULS	GLS	ML
λ_{11}	1.000	1.000	1.000
λ_{21}	0.188	0.205	0.205
λ_{32}	1.000	1.000	1.000
λ_{42}	0.268	0.270	0.271
ϕ_{11}	1.938	1.800	1.781
ϕ_{22}	1.424	1.431	1.408
ϕ_{12}	1.051	1.046	1.045
θ_{11}	0.164	0.300	0.322
θ_{22}	0.239	0.220	0.233
θ_{33}	0.480	0.467	0.497
θ_{44}	0.150	0.141	0.150
$COR(\xi_1, \xi_2)$	0.633	0.652	0.660
$REL(\xi_1, x_1)$	0.922	0.857	0.847
$REL(\xi_1, x_2)$	0.222	0.286	0.244
$REL(\xi_2, x_3)$	0.748	0.755	0.739
$REL(\xi_2, x_4)$	0.407	0.443	0.407
df	1	1	1
Chi-square	−	17.32	18.31
prob	−	0.000	0.000

NOTE: Underlines indicate those parameters that have been constrained to equal the given value.

correlation between the number of psychophysiological symptoms is 0.31 (see Appendix I). The attenuation in the correlation between the observed variables has been eliminated in the estimation of the correlation between the latent variables.

The second parameter of interest is the reliability of the observed variables. The reliability is defined as the squared correlation between a latent variable and its observed indicator. As such it indicates the percentage of variation in an observed variable that is explained by the common factor that it is intended to measure. To illustrate the computation of reliabilities, consider the observed variable x_2, which is a measure of ξ_1. The factor equation for x_2 is $x_2 = \lambda_{21}\xi_1 + \delta_2$. Since the variables are measured as deviations from their means, $COV(\xi_1, x_2) = E[\xi_1 x_2] = E[\xi_1(\lambda_{21}\xi_1 + \delta_2)]$. Using the fact that ξ_1 and δ_2 are assumed uncorrelated, $COV(\xi_1,x_2) = \lambda_{21}\phi_{11}$. Since the correlation between x_2 and ξ_1 is the covariance divided by the standard deviations of x_2 and ξ_1, the squared correlation or reliability is defined as

$$REL(\xi_1,x_2) = (\lambda_{21}\phi_{11})^2 / (\sigma_{22}\phi_{11})$$

$$= \lambda_{21}^2\phi_{11}/\sigma_{22}$$

See Sullivan and Feldman (1979), Bagozzi (1981), and Kenny (1979) for details on the computation of reliabilities in other types of models.

The reliabilities computed for M_d are given in Table 5.1 for each method of estimation. The measures of psychological symptoms (x_1 and x_3) are much more reliable than the measures of psychophysiological symptoms (x_2 and x_4) for all methods of estimation. One might conclude that this is due to the fixed loadings linking x_1 to ξ_1 and x_3 to ξ_2. This is not the case, however, as is demonstrated by considering alternative methods for setting the metric.

Table 5.2 presents ML estimates of M_d for five different ways of setting the scale. For the model just considered, the scale is set by fixing λ_{11} and λ_{32} to equal 1.0. The scale of ξ_1 is determined by x_1 and the scale of ξ_2 by x_3. Differences in the variables x_1 and x_3 are reflected in the different variances of ξ_1 ($\phi_{11} = 1.78$) and ξ_2 ($\phi_{22} = 1.41$). The factor correlations and reliabilities for this model were discussed above. This version of M_d will be referred to as M_{d1}.

In a second version of M_d, M_{d2}, the scale is set by fixing to 1.0 the loadings of ξ_1 on x_2 and ξ_2 on x_4. While the estimates of Λ and Φ differ from those for M_{d1}, the chi-square, the correlation between ξ_1 and ξ_2, and the reliabilities are the same. The change in the loadings simply reflects a change in the scale of the common factors. To see this, consider the effect on x_1 of a one-standard deviation change in ξ_1. For M_{d1} this involves a change in ξ_1 of 1.335 ($= \sqrt{\phi_{11}}$) . The increase in x_1 equals 1.335 times the loading of x_1 on ξ_1 ($= 1.00$), or an increase of 1.335. For M_{d2} a standard deviation increase in ξ_1 equals 0.274 ($= \sqrt{\phi_{11}}$) . The increase in x_1 equals 0.274 times the loading of x_1 on ξ_3 ($= 4.874$), or an increase of 1.335. Thus, the larger variances of the latent variables in M_{d1} as opposed to M_{d2} are exactly compensated for by the smaller loadings in M_{d1}.

TABLE 5.2
ML Estimates of M_d with Different Constraints to Set the Metric

Parameter	Model Estimated				
	M_{d1}	M_{d2}	M_{d3}	M_{d4}	M_{d5}
λ_{11}	<u>1.000</u>	4.874	<u>2.000</u>	1.335	0.944
λ_{21}	0.205	<u>1.000</u>	0.410	0.274	0.194
λ_{32}	<u>1.000</u>	3.694	<u>2.000</u>	1.187	0.839
λ_{42}	0.271	<u>1.000</u>	0.541	0.321	0.227
ϕ_{11}	1.781	0.075	0.445	<u>1.000</u>	<u>2.000</u>
ϕ_{22}	1.408	0.103	0.352	<u>1.000</u>	<u>2.000</u>
ϕ_{12}	1.045	0.058	0.261	0.660	1.320
θ_{11}	0.322	0.322	0.322	0.322	0.322
θ_{22}	0.233	0.233	0.233	0.233	0.233
θ_{33}	0.497	0.497	0.497	0.497	0.497
θ_{44}	0.150	0.150	0.150	0.150	0.150
$COR(\xi_1, \xi_2)$	0.660	0.660	0.660	0.660	0.660
$REL(\xi_1, x_1)$	0.847	0.847	0.847	0.847	0.847
$REL(\xi_1, x_2)$	0.244	0.244	0.244	0.244	0.244
$REL(\xi_2, x_3)$	0.739	0.739	0.739	0.739	0.739
$REL(\xi_2, x_4)$	0.407	0.407	0.407	0.407	0.407
df	1	1	1	1	1
Chi-square	18.31	18.31	18.31	18.31	18.31
prob	0.000	0.000	0.000	0.000	0.000

NOTE: Underlines indicate those parameters that have been constrained to equal the given value.

Model M_{d3} illustrates that the scale can also be set by fixing one loading on each factor to any constant. In this case the loadings are arbitrarily fixed to 2.0. The chi-square, the factor correlation, and the reliabilities are unchanged. Differences in other parameters simply reflect changes in scale.

Often it is convenient to directly set the scale of the common factors by fixing the diagonal of Φ. In model M_{d4} this is done by standardizing the factors to unit variance, and in model M_{d5} by standardizing to a variance of 2.0. The only differences in these models are the scale of the latent variables and the compensating changes in the magnitudes of the loadings.

In general, changes in the scale of the common factors do not affect the substantive results of the analyses. An exception to this rule occurs when equality constraints are used. This topic is discussed below.

While M_d is useful for demonstrating the interpretation of various parameters in the model and the basic ideas of establishing metrics, its fit is not adequate, as indicated by the chi-square of 18.3 with one degree of freedom. To improve the fit, coefficients that are not statistically different from zero can be considered for dropping from the model. In column 2 of Table 5.3 the z-values for each parameter in M_d are given. All are statistically significant beyond the .0001 level, except for the parameter θ_{11}. To fix this parameter to zero, while statistically convenient, does not make substantive sense. Accordingly, other types of constraints should be considered.

Since the model includes the same variables measured at two points in time, it might be reasonable to assume that both the loadings of the observed variables on the common factors and the variances of the common factors are identical at both points. This corresponds to assuming that $\lambda_{11} = \lambda_{32}$, $\lambda_{21} = \lambda_{42}$, and $\phi_{11} = \phi_{22}$. Since λ_{11} and λ_{32} are already constrained to equal 1.0, they are implicitly constrained to be equal. Thus, only two constraints are being added, with a gain of two degrees of freedom. The resulting model, designated as M_g in our earlier discussion (see Table 3.1), has a chi-square of 22.57 with three degrees of freedom. To test the hypothesis H_0: $\lambda_{21} = \lambda_{42}$ and $\phi_{11} = \phi_{22}$, a difference of chi-square test comparing M_d and M_g can be computed. The resulting chi-square is 4.21 with two degrees of freedom, and the hypothesis cannot be rejected at the .10 level of significance. The constraints are supported by the data.

It may also be possible to improve the fit by freeing parameters. In M_g the maximum modification index is 15.09 for θ_{42}. This means that if θ_{42} is freed, the minimum decrease in the chi-square will be 15.09 with a loss of one degree of freedom. The model formed by freeing θ_{42} is labeled M_h (see the broken and solid arrows in Figure 5.1) and was proven identified in Chapter 3; hence, it may be estimated. The actual improvement in fit is 16.71, which is highly significant, although the overall fit of the model is marginal with a chi-square of 5.86 with two degrees of freedom and a probability level of .053.

The maximum modification index for M_h is 3.19 for λ_{22}. Relaxing this parameter would allow the number of psychophysiological symp-

TABLE 5.3
ML Estimates of M_d, M_g, and M_h

Parameter	M_d Estimate	z-value	M_g Estimate	z-value	M_h Estimate	z-value
λ_{11}	1.000	–	1.000	–	1.000	–
λ_{21}	0.205	7.88	0.244[A]	13.69	0.227[A]	12.14
λ_{32}	1.000	–	1.000	–	1.000	–
λ_{42}	0.271	11.14	0.244[A]	13.69	0.227[A]	12.14
ϕ_{11}	1.781	7.88	1.538[B]	11.68	1.658[B]	11.90
ϕ_{22}	1.408	9.30	1.538[B]	11.68	1.658[B]	11.90
ϕ_{12}	1.045	11.36	1.038	11.32	1.046	11.39
θ_{11}	0.322	1.67	0.519	4.44	0.412	3.33
θ_{22}	0.233	14.88	0.225	15.12	0.230	15.34
θ_{33}	0.497	4.43	0.405	3.77	0.271	2.23
θ_{44}	0.150	12.78	0.156	14.06	0.163	14.42
θ_{42}	0.000	–	0.000	–	0.035	4.04
df	1		3		2	
Chi-square	18.31		22.57		5.86	
prob	0.000		0.000		0.053	

NOTE: Underlines indicate those parameters that have been constrained to equal the given value. As are values constrained to be equal; Bs are values constrained to be equal.

toms at time 1 (x_2) to load on the psychological disorder factor at time 2 (ξ_2). Since this makes no substantive sense, relaxing λ_{22} should not be considered. The second-largest modification index is for θ_{41}, which is also substantively inappropriate to relax. The third-largest modification index is for θ_{31}, which does make substantive sense, indicating correlated errors in measurement of the same variable measured at two points in time. If this parameter were relaxed, the resulting model (which adds the parameter θ_{31} to M_h) is not identified. Accordingly, the specification search ends.

The final model, M_h, was constructed through an exploratory search. Even though the search was guided by substantive considerations, the resulting parameter estimates and statistical tests must be viewed with caution. Ideally, the model should be verified with an independent sample. //

Standardization

A final issue to consider is standardization, which has two distinct meanings in the factor model. First, the *observed* variables can be standardized so that S is a correlation matrix rather than a covariance matrix. Second, the *latent* variables can be standardized by constraining the diagonal elements of Φ to equal one. These two meanings of standardization are linked through the concept of scale invariance which can be illustrated by reconsidering models M_d and M_g.

Table 5.4 contains four sets of parameters for M_d. In column 1 the metric is established by the fixed loadings on $\lambda_{11} = \lambda_{32} = 1.0$, and the observed variables are unstandardized. That is, a covariance matrix rather than a correlation matrix is analyzed. In column 2 the metric is established by the fixed variances of ξ_1 and ξ_2, and the observed variables are unstandardized. In both cases the chi-square is 18.31 with one degree of freedom. Further, the parameters are the same except for the change in scale. For example, the loading of x_1 on ξ_1 in column 1 is fixed at 1.0; in column 2 the loading is estimated to be 1.335. These differences are offset by the differences in the variances of ξ_1. For column 1, the standard deviation of ξ_1 is 1.335 ($= \sqrt{\phi_{11}}$), compared to the fixed standard deviation of 1.0 in column 2. Accordingly, a change in the latent variable of some fixed amount Δ in column 1 corresponds to a change of $\Delta/1.335$ in column 2. For both versions of M_d the resulting change in the observed variable is the same.

In columns 3 and 4 comparable results are presented for the analysis of the correlation matrix rather than the covariance matrix; that is, the observed variables have been standardized. Column 3 has λ_{11} and λ_{32} fixed to 1.0; column 4 has fixed variances for ξ_1 and ξ_2. The correlations between ξ_1 and ξ_2, the reliabilities, and the chi-squares are the same for all versions of M_d. Differences in Λ and Φ simply reflect the differences in the scales of the observed variables and common factors.

For M_d the decision to analyze the covariance matrix as opposed to the correlation matrix, or to set the metric by fixing loadings as opposed to fixing variances, makes no substantive difference when a scale-free estimator (such as ML or GLS) is used. These results would not hold, however, if a method such as ULS, which is scale dependent, were used.

TABLE 5.4

ML Estimates of M_d and M_g with Standardized Observed
Variables and/or Standardized Common Factors

	Model M_d				Model M_g			
O.V. Standardized?[a]	no	no	yes	yes	no	no	yes	yes
L.V. Standardized?[b]	no	yes	no	yes	no	yes	no	yes
Parameter								
λ_{11}	1.000	1.335	1.000	0.920	1.000	1.240[B]	1.000	0.885[B]
λ_{21}	0.205	0.274	0.536	0.493	0.244[A]	0.303[A]	0.645[A]	0.571[A]
λ_{32}	1.000	1.187	1.000	0.860	1.000	1.240[B]	1.000	0.885[B]
λ_{42}	0.271	0.321	0.743	0.639	0.244[A]	0.303[A]	0.645[A]	0.571[A]
ϕ_{11}	1.782	1.000	0.847	1.000	1.538[B]	1.000	0.782[B]	1.000
ϕ_{22}	1.408	1.000	0.739	1.000	1.538[B]	1.000	0.782[B]	1.000
ϕ_{12}	1.045	0.660	0.522	0.660	1.038	0.675	0.522	0.667
θ_{11}	0.322	0.322	0.153	0.153	0.519	0.519	0.222	0.222
θ_{22}	0.233	0.233	0.757	0.757	0.225	0.225	0.733	0.733
θ_{33}	0.497	0.497	0.261	0.261	0.405	0.405	0.213	0.213
θ_{44}	0.150	0.150	0.592	0.592	0.156	0.156	0.623	0.623
VAR(x_1)	2.102	2.102	1.000	1.000	2.102	2.102	1.000	1.000
VAR(x_2)	0.308	0.308	1.000	1.000	0.308	0.308	1.000	1.000
VAR(x_3)	1.904	1.904	1.000	1.000	1.904	1.904	1.000	1.000
VAR(x_4)	0.253	0.253	1.000	1.000	0.253	0.253	1.000	1.000
COR(ξ_1,ξ_2)	0.660	0.660	0.660	0.660	0.675	0.675	0.667	0.667
REL(ξ_1,x_1)	0.847	0.847	0.847	0.847	0.753	0.753	0.778	0.778
REL(ξ_1,x_2)	0.244	0.244	0.244	0.244	0.269	0.269	0.267	0.267
REL(ξ_2,x_3)	0.739	0.739	0.739	0.739	0.787	0.787	0.787	0.787
REL(ξ_2,x_4)	0.407	0.407	0.407	0.407	0.383	0.383	0.377	0.377
df	1	1	1	1	3	3	3	3
Chi-square	18.31	18.31	18.31	18.31	22.57	22.57	24.59	24.59

NOTE: Underlines indicate those parameters that have been constrained to equal
the given value. As are values constrained to be equal; Bs are values constrained to
be equal.
a. O.V. = observed variables.
b. L.V. = latent variables.

Quite different results are found in analyzing M_g. Recall that M_g
differs from M_d in that the equality constraints $\phi_{11} = \phi_{22}$, $\lambda_{11} = \lambda_{32}$, and
$\lambda_{21} = \lambda_{42}$ have been imposed. The choice of how to establish the metric
of the common factors in M_g has no substantive effect, as was the case in

M_d. The reader is encouraged to verify this using the estimates in columns 5 and 6. The choice of whether or not to standardize the observed variables, however, affects the substantive results obtained, even though a scale-free method of estimation is used. The models in columns 5 and 7 of Table 5.4 differ from one another only in the standardization of the observed variables in column 7. While such standardization did not affect the results for M_d, in M_g the chi-squares, reliabilities, and correlations between common factors differ. This is a consequence of the imposed equality constraints.

To standardize the observed variables and hence, Σ, requires the pre- and post-multiplication of the covariance equation $\Sigma = \Lambda\Phi\Lambda' + \Theta$ by a diagonal matrix D, where $d_{ii} = 1/\sqrt{s_{ii}}$ and s_{ii} is the variance of x_i. The resulting covariance equation is $D\Sigma D = (D\Lambda)\,\Phi\,(D\Lambda)' + D\Theta D$. Thus Λ changes from

$$\Lambda = \begin{bmatrix} 1 & 0 \\ \lambda_{21} & 0 \\ 0 & 1 \\ 0 & \lambda_{21} \end{bmatrix} \quad \text{to } D\Lambda = \begin{bmatrix} d_{11} & 0 \\ d_{22}\lambda_{21} & 0 \\ 0 & d_{33} \\ 0 & d_{44}\lambda_{21} \end{bmatrix}$$

where the underlined values are constants that have been fixed in the specification of the model. The only way that the equality constraints in Λ can be maintained in $D\Lambda$ is if $d_{11} = d_{33}$ and $d_{22} = d_{44}$, which will not be true unless $s_{11} = s_{33}$ and $s_{22} = s_{44}$. Unless these variances are equal in the sample (which is almost certainly not the case), scale invariance must be given up in order to maintain the imposed equality constraints. In the current example the loss of scale invariance does not have a major effect on the results obtained since the variances of x_1 and x_3, and x_2 and x_4 are similar in the sample data. As a general rule, however, in the presence of equality constraints the decision to analyze the correlation matrix as opposed to the covariance matrix can have significant substantive effects on the results obtained. In general it is preferable to analyze the covariance matrix.

6. CONCLUSIONS

The confirmatory factor model is a powerful statistical model. Its ability to test specific structures suggested by substantive theory gives it a major advantage over the exploratory factor model. The examples presented in Chapters 1 through 5 are quite simple, having the advantage of allowing a relatively simple presentation of the basic concepts and techniques. The reader should not be left with the impression, however, that more complex models cannot be analyzed. Complexities can be readily added by increasing the number of observed variables, common factors, correlations among error factors, and factor loadings. While the resulting models are more complex, the issues of specification, identification, estimation, and hypothesis testing are unchanged.

For the interested reader the following applications are recommended as examples of the flexibility of the model.

(1) Bagozzi (1981) gave a detailed presentation of the use of the confirmatory factor model for studying validity and reliability.

(2) Jöreskog (1969) presented the statistical justification of the confirmatory factor model and details on numerical issues related to estimation, along with a number of examples. The paper is mathematically demanding.

(3) Jöreskog and Sörbom (1981) is the manual accompanying LISREL V. The example on pages III.1-III.21 provides an extensive discussion of the interpretation of a confirmatory factor model.

(4) Kenny (1979) is useful in a number of respects. Early chapters develop the algebraic techniques necessary for proving that a model is identified. While many of the models considered in the book cannot be incorporated into the confirmatory factor model, most of those presented in Chapters 7 and 8 can. Recasting these models into the framework presented in this monograph and then estimating them is a useful exercise.

(5) Sullivan and Feldman (1979) considered a variety of models for multiple indicators, including the MMMT model. Most of these models can be estimated with the confirmatory factor model, which would also be a useful exercise.

(6) Zeller and Carmines (1980) considered the general issue of measurement in the social sciences. Their Appendix demonstrates how many of these issues can be addressed with the confirmatory factor model. Note in particular pages 176-184.

The reader is strongly encouraged to consult these sources and the references they contain. The best way to obtain a clear understanding of the confirmatory factor model is to study applications and to apply the model to actual data. The above references are extremely useful in both respects.

Even with the flexibility of the confirmatory factor model and its advantage over the exploratory factor model, it is limited by its inability to incorporate structural relationships among common factors and by a lack of provisions for qualitative data. Both of these limitations can, however, be overcome by extensions of the basic model.

Qualitative data can be handled in two ways. First, confirmatory factor models can be compared across populations. This essentially involves the simultaneous estimation of confirmatory factor models for different groups, and the testing of the hypothesis that the factor structures are the same in all groups. Jöreskog (1971), Sörbom (1974), and Werts et al. (1979) discussed this extension of the model. Second, the observed, x-variables can be categorical. This extension of the model, recently proposed by Jöreskog and Sörbom (1981: chap. 4), involves computations of polychoric, tetrachoric, and polyserial correlations.

To analyze structural relations among common factors requires the unification of the confirmatory factor model (CFM) and the structural equation model. This important extension is accomplished in the covariance structure model, sometimes referred to as the LISREL model. This is the subject of the companion volume in this series, *Covariance Structure Models*.

APPENDIX I

Correlations and Standard Deviations from
Wheaton/Hennepin Sample (N = 63)

Variables	PSY67	PHY67	PSY71	PHY71
PSY67	1.000			
PHY67	0.454	1.000		
PSY71	0.526	0.247	1.000	
PSY71	0.377	0.309	0.549	1.000
S.D.	1.45	0.555	1.38	0.503

SOURCE: Wheaton (1978: 395).

Variable Identifications:
PSY67 = psychological disorders 1967 (x_1)
PHY67 = psychophysiological disorders 1967 (x_2)
PSY71 = psychological disorders 1971 (x_3)
PHY71 = psychophysiological disorders 1971 (x_4)

APPENDIX II: SOFTWARE TO ESTIMATE THE
CONFIRMATORY FACTOR MODEL (CFM)

In general, the easiest way to estimate the CFM is with software designed for the covariance structure model. LISREL (versions I through V) and MILS (Schoenberg, 1982b) are the most commonly available programs. Information on obtaining LISREL can be obtained from International Educational Services, 1525 East 53rd Street, Suite 829, Chicago, IL 60615. Information on obtaining MILS can be obtained from Dr. Ronald Schoenberg, National Institutes of Health, Bldg. 31, Room 4C11, Bethesda, MD 20205. To understand how to estimate the CFM using the more general covariance structure model, it is necessary to briefly describe the covariance structure model. More details can be found in the companion volume in this series, *Covariance Structure Models*.

The covariance structure model consists of three matrix equations:

$$\mathbf{x} = \Lambda_x \xi + \delta \qquad \text{[II.1]}$$

$$\mathbf{y} = \Lambda_y \eta + \epsilon \qquad \text{[II.2]}$$

$$\eta = B\eta + \Gamma\xi + \zeta \qquad\qquad [\text{II.3}]$$

This last equation is sometimes written as

$$\ddot{B}\eta = \Gamma\xi + \zeta \qquad\qquad [\text{II.3}']$$

$\ddot{B} = (I - B)$. x and y are vectors of observed variables. η and ξ contain common factors. Φ is the covariance matrix for ξ. δ, ϵ, and ζ contain error factors, with covariance matrices Θ_δ, Θ_ϵ, and Ψ, respectively.

The CFM can be formed by imposing the following constraints:

$$B = 0 \ (\text{or } \ddot{B} = I) \qquad \Lambda_y = 0$$

$$\Gamma = 0 \qquad\qquad\qquad \Theta_\epsilon = 0 \qquad\qquad [\text{II.4}]$$

$$\Psi = 0$$

This, in effect, eliminates equations II.2 and II.3. Equation II.1, along with the covariance matrices Φ and Θ_δ, can be used to estimate the CFM. The x in our presentation corresponds to the x in equation II.1. Λ_x corresponds to our Λ. ξ corresponds to our ξ. Φ corresponds to our Φ. Finally, Θ_δ corresponds to our Θ.

NOTES

1. The symbol "//" will be used to designate the end of an example.

2. Equation 2.4 requires two matrix operations: addition and multiplication. Matrix addition requires that the two matrices to be added are of the same dimension. This means that they must have the same number of rows and columns. For example, adding the (3×2) matrices A and B results in

$$A + B = \begin{bmatrix} 1 & 2 \\ 3 & 4 \\ 5 & 6 \end{bmatrix} \begin{bmatrix} 7 & 8 \\ 9 & 10 \\ 11 & 12 \end{bmatrix} = \begin{bmatrix} 1{+}7 & 2{+}8 \\ 3{+}9 & 4{+}10 \\ 5{+}11 & 6{+}12 \end{bmatrix}$$

Assume that we want to multiply C of dimension $(q \times r)$ by D of dimension $(s \times t)$: CD. Matrix multiplication requires that the number of columns in the first matrix equal the number of rows in the second matrix, or for multiplying **CD**, that r = s. The other dimensions need not be equal. The resulting matrix will be of dimension (q × t). For example, if **C** is (2 × 3) and **D** is (3 × 2):

$$
CD = \begin{bmatrix} 1 & 2 & 3 \\ 4 & 5 & 6 \end{bmatrix} \begin{bmatrix} 7 & 8 \\ 9 & 10 \\ 11 & 12 \end{bmatrix} = \begin{bmatrix} (1*7 + 2*9 + 3*11) & (1*8 + 2*10 + 3*12) \\ (4*7 + 5*9 + 6*11) & (4*8 + 5*10 + 6*12) \end{bmatrix}
$$

3. "E" is the expectation operator. If X is a random variable, E(X) is the expected value of X, or for our purposes, the mean of X. If **x** is a (q × 1) vector of random variables, E(**x**) is a (q × 1) vector containing the expected values or means of the random variables in **x**. When the expectation operator is applied to a matrix, the expected value of each element of the matrix is taken.

4. This assumption affects some types of analyses that compare factor models across populations, and particularly models with structured means. These models are beyond the scope of our presentation. For details, see Jöreskog (1971), Sörbom (1974, 1982), and Jöreskog and Sörbom (1981).

5. "COV" is the covariance operator. If X and Y are two random variables, COV(X,Y) indicates the covariance between X and Y. Recalling that the covariance between X and Y is the average of the product of the deviations of X and Y from their means, COV(X,Y) can be written as $E[(X - \mu_x)(Y - \mu_y)]$, where μ_x and μ_y are the means of X and Y.

6. " ' " indicates the transpose of a matrix. Transposing involves taking rows of a matrix and standing them on end to make them columns. For example, consider **A**, a (2 × 3) matrix. If

$$
A = \begin{bmatrix} 1 & 2 & 3 \\ 4 & 5 & 6 \end{bmatrix}
$$

then

$$
A' = \begin{bmatrix} 1 & 4 \\ 2 & 5 \\ 3 & 6 \end{bmatrix}
$$

7. Some programs for estimating the confirmatory factor model do not allow the unique factors to be correlated. This is not a real limitation since unique factors can be

allowed to correlate in these programs by treating them as though they are common factors that load on only one observed variable and that are uncorrelated with the "real" common factors. For details on making this change, see Long (1981).

8. To count the unique elements of a covariance matrix it is necessary to keep in mind that the matrix is symmetric. For Σ, a $(q \times q)$ covariance matrix, this means that if σ_{ij} is counted, σ_{ji} should not be counted (for $i \neq j$). The unique elements can be counted as follows: Of the q^2 elements in Σ, the q diagonal elements are variances. The remaining $q^2 - q$ elements are covariances, half of which are redundant. Thus, there are $q + (q^2 - q)/2 = q(q + 1)/2$ unique elements in Σ.

9. A square matrix A of dimension $(r \times r)$ is said to be invertible or nonsingular if there exists a square matrix A^{-1} of dimension $(r \times r)$, such that $AA^{-1} = I$, where I is a $(r \times r)$ identity matrix.

10. In exploratory factor analysis equation 3.2 is generally replaced by $\Sigma = \Lambda\Lambda' + \Theta$. This involves assuming that $\Phi = I$, or that the factors are orthogonal. This does not really constrain the exploratory model since the assumption is relaxed after estimation, when factor rotations are made (see, Lawley and Maxwell, 1971: 66-86).

11. If X is a real, symmetric matrix of dimension $(r \times r)$ and a is any $(r \times 1)$ vector, X is positive definite if $a'Xa > 0$ for all possible a. All variance/covariance matrices are positive definite (Kmenta, 1971: 606).

12. A submatrix of A is defined as a matrix formed from A by deleting one or more rows and/or columns of A. The rank of a matrix is defined as the size of the largest nonsingular submatrix contained in A.

13. The technical problem with computational methods for determining whether a model is identified is that identification is a property of the specification of a model, not of the estimation of a model. If a model appears to be identified for a particular set of estimates based on the positive definiteness of the information matrix, this may result from having drawn an unusual sample rather than from the fact that the model is identified. For a more technical discussion of this issue, see Schoenberg (1982a) and McDonald and Krane (1979).

14. The fitting function for unweighted least squares is sometimes written as $F_{ULS} = \frac{1}{2}tr[(S - \hat{\Sigma})^2]$, dividing the function given in the text by $\frac{1}{2}$. This change in scale does not affect the values obtained as estimates of Λ, Φ, and Θ.

15. The fitting function for generalized least squares is often written as $F_{GLS} = \frac{1}{2}tr[(S - \Sigma^*)S^{-1}]^2$. The difference in scale caused by the multiplication by $\frac{1}{2}$ will not affect the values of the estimates obtained.

16. The determinant of a square matrix can be defined as follows. Consider a square matrix, say X, of order $(r \times r)$, with individual elements designated as x_{ij}. The determinant of X is defined as

$$|X| = \Sigma \pm x_{1j_1} x_{2j_2} \ldots x_{rj_r}$$

where the sum is over permutations of the second subscript, and the sign is positive for even permutations and negative for odd permutations. For example, if X is a (2×2) matrix, $|X| = x_{11}x_{22} - x_{12}x_{21}$. If X is a (3×3) matrix, $|X| = x_{11}x_{22}x_{33} - x_{12}x_{21}x_{33} + x_{12}x_{23}x_{31} - x_{13}x_{22}x_{31} + x_{13}x_{21}x_{32} - x_{11}x_{23}x_{32}$. For more details, see Hohn (1973).

17. The fitting function for maximum likelihood estimation is often written in the alternative form: $F_{ML} = tr(S\Sigma^{-1}) + [log|\Sigma^*| - log|S|]$. This function differs from the text by the subtraction of q, where q is the number of independent variables. This is only a change in origin of the function which will not affect the values of the parameters that minimize the function. The function in the text is used since it has a close relationship to

the computation of the chi-square statistic discussed in Chapter 5. The fitting function is sometimes simplified by making use of the equality log $|\Sigma^{-1}S| = \log|S| - \log|\Sigma|$, resulting in $F_{ML} = \text{tr}(S\Sigma^{*-1} - \log|\Sigma^{*-1}S| - q$.

18. If a model is just identified, closed-form solutions can be obtained by solving the covariance equations for each parameter.

19. This z-statistic is labeled as a t-statistic in the program LISREL and in many applications of the confirmatory factor model. It does not, however, have a t-distribution.

20. In an exploratory search there is generally a class of parameters that could reasonably be included in the model, although there is no strong substantive reason for either including them or excluding them. On the other hand, there is usually another class of parameters that make no substantive sense. Parameters from this second class should not be freed, even if the modification index suggests that freeing one of them will result in the maximum improvement of fit in the model. Little is gained if a model is constructed that reproduces the observed data but can be given no substantive interpretation.

21. Estimates were obtained using MILS (Schoenberg, 1982b) and LISREL V (Jöreskog and Sörbom, 1981).

REFERENCES

ALWIN, D. F. (1974) "Approaches to the interpretation of relationships in the multitrait-multimethod matrix," pp.79-105 in H. L. Costner (ed.) Sociological Methodology 1973-1974. San Francisco: Jossey-Bass.

BAGOZZI, R. P. (1981) "An examination of the validity of two models of attitude." Multivariate Behavioral Research 16: 323-359.

BENTLER, P. M. and D. G. BONETT (1980) "Significance tests and goodness-of-fit in the analysis of covariance structures." Psychological Bulletin 88: 588-606.

BENTLER, P. M. and D. G. WEEKS (1980) "Linear structural equations with latent variables." Psychometrika 45: 289-308.

BIELBY, W. T. and R. M. HAUSER (1977) "Response error in earning functions for nonblack males." Sociological Methods and Research 6: 241-280.

BLALOCK, H. M. (1979) Social Statistics. New York: McGraw-Hill.

BOOMSMA, A. (1982) "The robustness of LISREL against small sample sizes in factor analysis models," pp. 149-173 in H. Wold and K. Jöreskog (eds.) Systems Under Indirect Observation. New York: Elsevier North-Holland.

BROWNE, M. W. (1974) "Generalized least-squares estimators in the analysis of covariance structures." South African Statistical Journal 8: 1-24.

BURT, R. S., M. G. .FISCHER, and K. P. CHRISTMAN (1979) "Structures of well-being: sufficient conditions for identification in restricted covariance models." Sociological Methods and Research 8: 111-120.

BURT, R. S., J. A. WILEY M. J. MINOR, and J. R. MURRAY (1978) " Structures of well-being." Sociological Methods and Research 6: 365-407.

DUNCAN, O. D. (1975) Introduction to Structural Equation Models. New York: Academic.

DUNN, J. E. (1973) "A note on a sufficiency condition for uniqueness of a restricted factor matrix." Psychometrika 38: 141-143.

87

HARMON, H. H. (1976) Modern Factor Analysis. Chicago: University of Chicago Press.

HAYS, W. L. (1981) Statistics. New York: Holt, Rinehart & Winston.

HERTEL, B. R. (1976) "Minimizing error variance introduced by missing data routines in survey analysis." Sociological Methods and Research 4: 459-474.

HOHN, F. E. (1973) Elements of Matrix Analysis. New York: Macmillan.

HOWE, H. G. (1955) Some Contributions to Factor Analysis. Report ORNL-1919. Oak Ridge, TN: Oak Ridge National Laboratory.

JENNRICH, R. I. (1978) "Rotational equivalence of factor loading matrices with specified values." Psychometrika 43: 421-426.

JÖRESKOG, K. G. (1979) "Author's addendum to: A general approach to confirmatory maximum likelihood factor analysis," pp. 40-43 in K. G. Jöreskog and D. Sörbom (eds.) Advances in Factor Analysis and Structural Equation Models. Cambridge, MA: Abt Books.

——— (1971) "Simultaneous factor analysis in several populations." Psychometrika 36: 409-426.

——— (1969) "A general approach to confirmatory factor analysis." Psychometrika 34: 183-202.

——— (1967) "Some contributions to maximum likelihood factor analysis." Psychometrika 34: 183-202.

——— and A. S. GOLDBERGER (1972) "Factor analysis by generalized least squares." Psychometrika 37: 243-260.

JÖRESKOG, K. G. and D. SÖRBOM (1981) LISREL V. User's Guide. Chicago: National Educational Resources.

——— (1978) LISREL IV. User's Guide. Chicago: National Educational Resources.

JUDGE, G. G., W. E. GRIFFITHS, R. C. HILL, and T. C. LEE (1980) The Theory and Practice of Econometrics. New York: John Wiley.

KENNY, D. A. (1979) Correlation and Causality. New York: John Wiley.

KMENTA, J. (1971) Elements of Econometrics. New York: Macmillan.

LAWLEY, D. N. and A. E. MAXWELL (1971) Factor Analysis as a Statistical Method. New York: American Elsevier.

LEAMER, E. E. (1978) Specification Searches. New York: John Wiley.

LEE, S. Y. (1977) "Some algorithms for covariance structure analysis." Ph.D. dissertation. University of California, Los Angeles.

LONG, J. S. (1981) "Estimation and hypothesis testing in linear models containing measurement error," pp. 209-256 in P. V. Marsden (ed.) Linear Models in Social Research. Beverly Hills, CA: Sage.

——— (1976) "Estimation and hypothesis testing in linear models containing measurement error." Sociological Methods and Research 5: 157-206.

McDONALD, R. P. and W. R. KRANE (1979) "A Monte Carlo study of local identifiability and degrees of freedom in the asymptotic likelihood ratio test." British Journal of Mathematical and Statistical Psychology 32: 121-132.

SCHOENBERG, R. (1982a) Identification and the Condition of the Information Matrix in Maximum Likelihood Estimation of Structural Equation Models. Working Paper. Washington, DC: National Institute of Mental Health.

——— (1982b) MILS: A Computer Program to Estimate the Parameters of Multiple Indicator Linear Structure Models. Bethesda, MD: National Institutes of Health.

SÖRBOM, D. (1982) "Structural equation models with structured means," pp. 183-195 in H. Wold and K. Jöreskog (eds.) Systems under Indirect Observation. New York: Elsevier North-Holland.

———— (1975) "Detection of correlated errors in longitudinal data." British Journal of Mathematical and Statistical Psychology 28: 138-151.

———— (1974)"A general method for studying differences in factor means and factor structure between groups." British Journal of Mathematical and Statistical Psychology 27: 229-239.

SULLIVAN, J. L. and S. FELDMAN (1979) Multiple Indicators. Beverly Hills, CA: Sage.

WERTS, C. E., K. G. JORESKOG, AND R. L. LINN (1973) "Identification and estimation in path analysis with unmeasured variables." American Journal of Sociology 73: 1469-1484.

WERTS, C. E., D. A. ROCK, and J. GRANDY (1979) "Confirmatory factor analysis applications." Multivariate Behavioral Research 14: 199-213.

WHEATON, B. (1978) "The sociogenesis of psychological disorder." American Journal of Sociology 73: 1469-403.

WONNACOT, R. J. and T. H. WONNACOTT (1979) Econometrics. New York: John Wiley.

ZELLER, R. A. and E. G. CARMINES (1980) Measurement in the Social Sciences. New York: Cambridge University Press.

J. SCOTT LONG is Associate Professor of Sociology at Washington State University. His recent publications, focusing on issues of scientific productivity and academic careers, have appeared in American Sociological Review, Social Studies of Science, *and* Sociological Methods and Research, *among others. He is the author of a companion volume to this University Paper:* Covariance Structure Models: An Introduction to LISREL.

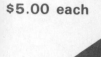

Quantitative Applications in the Social Sciences

in the Social Sciences

(a Sage University Papers Series)

$5.00 each

SAGE PUBLICATIONS, INC.
P.O. BOX 5024
BEVERLY HILLS, CALIFORNIA 90210